Why Doesn't GOD Do Things Perfectly?

D0921017

R. MAURICE BOYD

Why Doesn't GOD Do Things Perfectly?

I give you the end of a golden string;
Only wind it into a ball,
It will lead you in at Heaven's gate.
Built in Jerusalem's wall.

William Blake

ABINGDON PRESS
NASHVILLE

WHY DOESN'T GOD DO THINGS PERFECTLY?

Copyright © 1999 by Abingdon Press

All rights reserved.

No part of this work may be reproduced or transmitted in any form or by any means, electronic or mechanical, including photocopying and recording, or by any information storage or retrieval system, except as may be expressly permitted by the 1976 Copyright Act or in writing from the publisher. Requests for permission should be addressed to Abingdon Press, P.O. Box 801, Eighth Avenue South, Nashville, TN 37202-0801.

This book is printed on recycled, acid-free, elemental-chlorine–free paper.

Library of Congress Cataloging-in-Publication Data

Boyd, R. Maurice, 1932–
    Why doesn't God do things perfectly? / R. Maurice Boyd.
    p. cm.
    ISBN 0-687-07034-1 (alk. paper)
    1. Christian life. 2. Suffering—Religious aspects—Christianity. 3. Good and evil. 4. Theodicy. I. Title.
BV4501.2.B68337 1999
231'.8—dc21
                                       99-22991
                                         CIP

Scripture quotations, unless otherwise noted, are the author's paraphrase.

Scripture quotations noted NEB are from The New English Bible. © The Delegates of the Oxford University Press and the Syndics of the Cambridge University Press 1961, 1970. Reprinted by permission.

Scripture quotations noted KJV are from the King James Version of the Bible.

99 00 01 02 03 04 05 06 07 08—10 9 8 7 6 5 4 3 2 1

MANUFACTURED IN THE UNITED STATES OF AMERICA

FOR

Dora McLeer

"Now a long time in the Father's house."

CONTENTS

PREFACE

*T*he reason for this book is simple: I wish someone had told me years ago the things that are said in it. Maybe they did; perhaps they informed me of truths and presented me with insights which, by reason of immaturity, I could neither appreciate nor assimilate. But I do not think that they did, and that meant I had to discover them for myself.

There was some urgency about doing so. Shortly after I arrived at my first church, the loveliest girl in the town died a slow and painful death. Not yet sixteen years old, she was adored by all who knew her for her radiance of spirit and purity of heart. I could make no sense of her tragedy, either for myself or for those who had been tormented by her affliction, were bereft at her passing, and now looked to me for solace. Dora McLeer's death told me that if such a calamity could not be gathered into faith, it was not a faith I could either hold with integrity or preach with conviction.

That sad happening was fifty years ago, and the questions raised so poignantly by the sorrow of a young girl's passing, and by the bewilderment of those who loved her, have never left me. I do not know if what I say in this book will be helpful to you; I do know that the things written here are for me, and for others with whom I have shared them, "lamps for our gloom, hands guiding where we stumble" as we make our pilgrim way from "the land of lost content" to "the land of heart's desire."

R. Maurice Boyd
The City Church, New York
November 1998

CHAPTER ONE

"THE IMPORTANCE OF BEING EARNEST"

TROUBLING TROUBLE

Congratulations! You have already put your money, and are now putting your time and thought, where your complaint is. There are many who are not prepared to do that. They grumble about the world's ills, but are unwilling to think about them hard enough or long enough to either clarify their complaint or give it up. They remain obstinately superficial and settle into an attitude of undiscerning grievance.

WHAT THE BRIDE DID NOT HEAR

One Saturday afternoon I had a conversation with the best man as we waited in my vestry for the bride to arrive and her wedding to begin. He must have felt some pressure to talk religious talk, for he volunteered the information that he had once been a man of faith but had surrendered it in face of war, pestilence, and all the troubles of the world. His assured tone and arch demeanor suggested that he considered his position unassailable, that he thought himself more sensitive and more intelligent than those of us who still managed to keep a hold on faith in spite of the difficulties he mentioned. He seemed to think that his unbelief meant that he felt the world's anguish more keenly than believers did, that his mind was too perceptive to be persuaded by the explanations that satisfied those of us with smaller brains.

So I asked him how many books he had read on the subject of God and evil; and when he told me he had not read any, and had not talked to anyone about it at any great length or depth, I replied that his faith must not have meant much to him if he could surrender it so easily. He really ought not assume that in this matter he held the moral and intellectual high ground, for truth to tell, his skepticism lacked seriousness and would not enjoy much credibility among thoughtful people.

KEEPING FAITH IS WORTH THE TROUBLE

If his faith mattered enough for him to mention it to me, should he not have gone to a little trouble before giving it up? Being as well informed as he was, he must have known that keener minds and kinder hearts than his or mine had wrestled long and hard with the problem of evil and had better things to say about it than either of us had ever thought of. Did they not deserve a hearing? Did he feel the pain of the world more than, say, Mother Teresa? Had he thought about it with greater anguish than Job or Jesus; or more profoundly than Augustine or Aquinas or Kierkegaard; or in more menacing circumstances than Dietrich Bonhoeffer or Viktor Frankl?

Why was he so sure that there were no answers to his questions and that moral sensitivity, when matched by intellectual rigor, must lead to loss of faith? Might they not just as readily confirm and strengthen it? And how could he ever discover if these things were true without taking the trouble to find out?

The conversation having become more serious than he had bargained for, the young man began looking for a way out. The bride gave him one by arriving, only a little late, radiant and joyful, blissfully unaware of the pains of existence, totally convinced that this was the happiest of days in the best of all possible worlds.

EASY QUESTIONS, UNEASY ANSWERS

There are those who would rather hold on to their question than give it up for a good answer. It seems intelligent and sophisticated to question everything without having to answer anything, and it keeps them safely on the demand side rather than the supply side of the discussion. There is a fair use of questions that is wholly honorable, but there is also a questionable use of them that is evasive. We may keep on asking questions so as to avoid the claims of their answers.

I read of a man who, having struggled with the doubting part of himself for years, resolved that he would attend to the believing part of himself. He said that when he did so he moved from the agony of questions he could not answer to the anguish of answers he could not evade. Some of us choose to cling to our questions because we find complaint more easeful than faith and agnosticism more comfortable than belief.

WHY MY MOTHER WOULDN'T BUY THIS BOOK

My mother wouldn't buy this book because she wouldn't need to. As a dutiful son I would give her a copy bearing an expression of my affection and indebtedness. And if I were to neglect that labor of love, she would, of course, buy the book because her son had written it. But she would not buy it out of any great need to wrestle with its subject. The problem of pain, suffering, and evil hardly engaged her mind. I think she never for a moment doubted the love of God or the goodness of life; and when things went wrong, as they frequently did for her, what was that but an opportunity for faithfulness and fortitude? And when the lives of others were troubled, what was there to do but try to help them with one good turn after another? The world's troubles were God's invitation to trust His goodness and comfort His world by putting our energies at His disposal. This could mean anything from money for missions to chicken soup for a sick neighbor. The problem was practical rather than theoretical and the solution pragmatic rather than intellectual. What more was needed than kindness and common sense? So, like the Savior she loved, she "went about doing good."

"PLATITUDES UNDONE"

Yet, for others, my mother's practical solution is not practicable, for it doesn't work. They are willing to admit that it is not enough to talk about distress without attempting to relieve it; if we were to do so we should be guilty, not only of a practical failure, but of a moral one.

Yet the problem of evil is for many the greatest obstacle to faith. It requires not only a pragmatic solution, but a moral and intellectual answer. They are willing to help all they can but are still unable to understand how God can be good and allow the world to be the way it is. Indeed, they sometimes tell us that if they understood better, their conviction would give them a more confident ground for action. They believe that something has to be thought, as well as done, about the anguish of the world.

When Holbrook Jackson wrote *Platitudes in the Making,* he sent a copy to his friend G. K. Chesterton, who wrote his responses and reactions in green pencil in the margins of the book and sent it back to the author. One of Holbrook's platitudes read, "Don't think—do!" to which Chesterton replied, "Do think. Do!"

But what if we were to both think and do? If we were to think clearly and act compassionately, might we not discover that thinking is a kind of doing and doing a way of thinking? We might find our reflection strengthening our conviction and our conviction deepening our compassion. We should then think as people of action and act as people of thought.

CHAPTER TWO

LIMITED OBJECTIVES

MYSTERY STORY

hen a friend of mine heard that I was writing this book, he remarked that it must be like writing a mystery story. Austin Farrer, the philosopher, theologian, and author of mystery stories who wrote the best book there is on the nature of evil and the meaning of suffering, and to whom I am deeply indebted on every page of this book, might have agreed with him. He tells us in one of his essays:

> We do not comprehend the world, and we are not going to. It is, and it remains for us, a confused mystery of light and dark.

Yet even though we may not expect to comprehend the world or rob it of its mystery, we may surely attempt to understand it a little better than we do. If we can resolve some of the obstinate questions that insinuate themselves between us and confident belief, we are not only making the enigma of the world a little more manageable, but are permitting the claims of faith to be felt.

WHY SHOULD THIS HAPPEN TO ME?

A friend of mine discovered the truth of this when his little son was injured at play. The wee fellow was rushed to hospital and taken immediately to the operating room. His father, whose wife had died just a year earlier, waited in torment to learn the extent of the little man's injuries. Deeply distraught, he found himself complaining, "Why should this happen to me?"

Then he remembered that his minister had once said to his congregation, "If troubles happen to anyone, why shouldn't they happen to me? If any heart is broken, why should it not be my heart? Should I expect life's troubles to pass me by just because I have faith? Evils are an offense, not only when they happen to me, but when they happen to anyone. And when they do happen to others, we should not react with disinterest, but respond with all the sympathy of an 'earth-born companion and fellow-mortal,' for their distress might just as easily have been our own." My friend found that this "hard" word, which at first appeared to be lacking in sympathy and tenderness, nevertheless strengthened him to deal with his anxiety and saved him from the self-pity that was robbing him of his courage.

We should recognize that there is a sunny side to doubt that sees it as both the assertion of skepticism and the cutting edge of faith. Our doubts are sometimes little more than the disquiet of a mind weary of platitudes, the restlessness of our hunger for insight, the beckoning of a truth waiting to be discovered. That is why Rilke can exhort us to be patient towards all that is unsolved in our hearts and try to love the questions themselves. That is what moved Dostoyevsky to declare that his hosanna had come forth from the crucible of his doubts.

"A STITCH IN TIME"

It is another worthwhile objective to encourage and enable people to consider the world's ills while they are still able to do so, when their days are not desperate, and when they can think things through unhurriedly. Freud warns us that we falsify our life by refusing to think of death until it is upon us, wiping us out, destroying all that we are and everything we had hoped for. It is too late to prepare for the hurts that come to most of us sooner or later when they have already come. Albert Camus said that we hate death because it "makes the lie definitive"—the lie that we have endless time in which to improve our mind, make our character, and complete our work.

It is a mistake to go shopping for shirts when you need them. Go a little sooner and you will have a much better chance of finding the cloth and cut and color you really want at a price you are willing to pay. When sailing, one does not wait for the storm to test the integrity of the boat; it is better to be as sure as we can be of its seaworthiness before we leave harbor and before rough weather hits. We should imitate the old Scot who said that he weathered the winter's furious rages because he had thatched his cottage in fair weather.

LIFE IN THE FAST LANE

The qualities of faith, hope, and love, for example, which hold out the best promise to bring us through, cannot be acquired overnight; they are possessed when patiently strengthened and steadily built up over the years. Deep truths are not bits of stuff lying around waiting to be picked up by the idly curious; they can become ours only by the drama of discovering and living them. We possess them by making them part of ourselves, by weaving them into the clothing of the soul. Profound matters cannot be rushed. Still waters run deep. If we move in the fast lane we should not set our heart on anything that takes time.

"SANS TEETH, SANS EYES, SANS TASTE, SANS EVERYTHING"

Dr. Leslie Weatherhead was once asked to visit an elderly man who was close to death and had expressed his need and desire for a word of strength and reassurance. Weatherhead went to see him, but found him hardly able to hear and barely able to think. The old man did manage to mutter his regret that he had never had time enough to give much thought to the meaning of his life, or of his death. A little later, on learning the man's age, Dr. Weatherhead calculated that he had lived through four thousand, nine hundred, sixty Sundays.

It has always seemed to me an unhappy irony that at funerals, when we are compelled by the nature of the occasion to look at illness or accident and death, and not turn away our eyes, the only way we can see is through a mist of tears. At the very time when ultimate questions of life, death, and destiny are raised inescapably, we are in no condition to deal with them. We are often too shattered by shock, or numbed by grief, or angry, or bitter, or despairing to consider the meaning of any of it. When the questions appear most urgent, all our circuits are busy, for we are completely taken up by the effort merely to keep going; the most we can manage each day is to win through till nightfall.

It is in these circumstances that we may be tempted to fall back on the clichés of what a friend of mine used to call "native-wit philosophy," the platitudes of the thoughtless who will tell us, for example, that everything is for the best (when it often isn't) or that our lost loved one will live forever by being remembered (how can mortal memory confer immortality?). These truisms, being untrue, are frequently mischievous; for they can cloak a saying that not only fails to comfort but distorts the very truth in which comfort may be found.

"DEATH AND THE MAIDEN"

Not long ago, someone said to a friend of mine, "God never sends us more than we can bear." The words were kindly meant, but they are not true. We know many who have been broken in life, and by life. What happens to us is sometimes more than we can bear.

Recently, I heard of a man who liked his hamburgers rare and cooked them that way for himself and his little girl. He became gravely ill, but recovered. His little darling died. Having lived with that for a while, he could live with it no longer, so he took his own life.

The words "God never sends us more than we can bear" were well intentioned when spoken to my friend. They were uttered as consolation and offered as comfort, but there is neither strength nor solace in them. The person who spoke them meant, no doubt, that God considers our limits before sending our afflictions. But what the words say is that if we can bear it, God will send it; and the more we can bear, the more He will send. The Almighty presses us almost to our limit, but stops just short of breaking us, that He may later press us more. If our strength increases, so does the number and so does the weight of our afflictions; the more we can endure, the more is heaped up and piled on for the good, I suppose, of our souls.

Now, what kind of God could be capable of such behavior; and who among us would wish to worship Him? To worship is to ascribe worth, but how can we ascribe worth and value to conduct for which we have nothing but contempt?

I am reminded of *Death and the Maiden,* the play by Ariel Dorfman, subsequently made into a movie, in which a physician practices his profession in a prison where political prisoners are interrogated. The doctor's responsibility is to keep them alive so that their captors can continue torturing them. He brings them safely through the night so that the dawn will bring them more pain. As he goes about his work, he listens with much delight to Schubert's exquisite string quartet, *Death and the Maiden.*

Such a view belongs in a Hardy novel ("the President of the Immortals had ended his sport with Tess") and finds a voice in more than one of his poems. Shakespeare can give perfect expression to it, as he can find perfect words for almost anything:

> As flies to wanton boys, are we to the gods;
> They kill us for their sport.

But I am loathe to accept it as the truth of Christian faith; for it tells us nothing about the God who, far from sending our troubles to torture us, sends us His Son to bear our griefs and carry our sorrows.

"TROUBLES, WHEN THEY COME"

The truth is that troubles are not sent; they come. And they come, not because God personally directs them to a particular individual with a specific address, but because we all live in the kind of world where bad things happen. And when they happen, it is never to anyone, anywhere, but must always be to someone, somewhere. But troubles are not sent; they come. And they come as impartially as the rain that falls on the just and the unjust and the sunlight that shines on good and bad alike.

To believe that suffering is sent makes every bit of suffering a problem for faith. If it is sent, then why has it been sent to me rather than to someone else? Is it because I am more wicked than others? Is it that I have done more to deserve it, and is it a sign of divine disapproval?

But if suffering is not sent, but comes, then it will come as readily to me as to anyone. My question will not ask why it comes to me, but why it should come to anyone. I will receive it as my share of the world's pain. Indeed, I may even be able to reduce the likelihood of its coming to me. If it is sent, then there isn't much I can do about it; but if it is something that comes, then I may be able to discover why it comes and how to order my life so that it is less likely to come to me. I may read the statistics, for example, and resolve to give up smoking. I may visit my physician and have the tests I have been putting off for too long. I may take a little walk, lose a little weight, eat a little less. There is nothing unfair about attempting to avoid troubles in this way, for anyone can try it.

THE CAUSE OF ACCIDENTS

The same may be said of accidents. They are not sent; they come. Strictly speaking, accidents are not caused; they happen. If they are caused in the usual sense of that word, then they are intended; and an accident that is intended is no accident. Someone once described an accident as an unhappy happening that God did not intend and man did not foresee. Yet we often speak of finding the cause of accidents. This may be a useful thing to do, for it may prevent the same accident from happening again. But finding what caused an accident simply means discovering how it happened, not who "caused" it in the sense of willing it to happen. If we were to discover that someone intended it to happen, then we should have to conclude that what we thought was an accident was not an accident but a deliberate act. It might be an act of mischief, or even a criminal act, as Inspector Columbo discovered every other week.

People, indeed, are sometimes held accountable for accidents they "caused" even though they did not intend them to happen. They may have caused them by carelessness, or irresponsibility. Sometimes they cause them by what we call "criminal negligence" and are held responsible for their irresponsibility.

This becomes clear if we think of the accident that killed Princess Diana and killed or injured the other occupants of the car in which she was riding. Some accounts have alleged that the tragedy was "caused" by the paparazzi who were chasing the limousine carrying the princess. Yet the paparazzi did not intend it to happen. What they intended was to cause you and me to buy their pictures and read their accounts of the celebrities they were pursuing.

Now, if this is the nature of accidents, we should not torture ourselves trying to determine why God "caused" them to happen to us or to someone we love. Some people blame accidents on God, as though He intended and deliberately sent them. We should not make every chance occurrence a problem for faith. Accidents are not caused by God or by anybody else. They happen. Accidents happen as randomly as troubles come. If they are deliberately sent, they are not accidents. We may still think that God is "criminally negligent" in the accidents that happen to us. That is a question we shall consider in a later chapter.

PROBLEM OR GIFT?

Another useful objective is simply to affirm the goodness of life in the face of all that troubles us. Father D'Arcy quite properly begins his book on the pain of this world and the providence of God by affirming that life is a gift of grace to be accepted with gratitude, not a problem to be received with perplexity and complaint. If we reduce our existence to the level of a conundrum to be solved rather than a benefit to be welcomed, then we are guilty of both blindness and ingratitude.

We sometimes allow ourselves to sink into believing that because life has its problems it is itself a problem, forgetting that life itself is greater than anything it brings to us. If we may suffer defeats without being defeated, and endure losses without being losers, then surely we can deal with life's difficulties without reducing life itself to a difficulty.

"TO BE, OR NOT TO BE?"

For all our complaining, we give ourselves away by bringing children into the world and believing it a good thing to do. We celebrate birthdays and reckon the year of our birth a very good year; indeed, we give and receive birthday gifts only because we believe that birth itself is a gift. We try to extend our own time as far as we can beyond the "threescore years and ten" of our allotted span, and boast of our accomplishment when we succeed in doing so. Our complaining is like that of the residents of the nursing home who in one and the same breath bewail both the quality of the food and the smallness of the portions.

The conviction that life is good informs our moral values, excites our moral expectations, and shapes our moral questions. Without it, there would be little debate about murder, war, abortion, assisted suicide, euthanasia, capital punishment, and a dozen other personal and social moral issues. It is because we believe life to be good that we put people in prison for taking it.

Indeed, life is perceived to be so precious that when some find it insupportable and choose to end it, we do not conclude that existence is bad and their action fitting; we are saddened to think that so much went so wrong as to make it unendurable. Hamlet thinks the question is "To be, or not to be?" but most of us, most of the time, think that a very odd question indeed. When we ponder whether "not to be" is better than "to be," we forget that it is only by being that we can ask the question in the first place.

"A LOVER'S QUARREL WITH THE WORLD"

Robert Frost once found himself wandering idly through a cemetery, looking at tombstones. As he walked, he read the dates and inscriptions, the engraved words that marked a coming and a going and sought to capture a life: born when, died where, and a terse phrase to sum up what happened in between. Frost asked himself what epitaph he would choose for his own gravestone, and decided that he wanted the words, "I had a lover's quarrel with the world."

It would be hard to live in this world and not have a quarrel with it. Yet it should be a lover's quarrel. Thomas Traherne put it splendidly by reminding us that we shall never enjoy the world aright "till we remember how lately we were made and how wonderful it was when we came into it." George Borrow comes to the same conclusion:

> Life is sweet, brother. Sweet, brother? There's night and day, brother, both sweet things; sun, moon, and stars, brother, all sweet things; there's likewise a wind on the heath. Life is very sweet, brother, who would wish to die?

ANSWERING THE MADMAN

Yet another of our limited objectives is to give some answer to those who not only turn from belief because of the existence of evil but may attack faith because of it. If they receive no answer to their objections, they may well conclude that it is because there are no answers; and the case for belief is lost by default. That is why Dag Hammarskjøld was alarmed by the shouts of the madman in the marketplace:

> No one stopped to answer him. Thus it was confirmed that his theses were incontrovertible.

Somebody once remarked that while one fool can ask more idle questions than a hundred wise men can answer, teachers, parents, and bishops must nevertheless answer them lest the idlers ensnare one innocent heart.

APOLOGETICS WITHOUT APOLOGY

Which brings us to our need for apologetics. When we speak of apologetics, some might easily imagine that we are talking about people who are so inordinately shy, and so chronically inferior, that they spend all their time telling everyone how sorry they are about everything. That is not what we mean by it. There are no "Apologetics Anonymous" groups organized to provide support for chronic apologizers; at least, if there are, we have not heard of them. Apologetics is not apology raised to the level of art, or reduced to the level of neurosis; it is the spirited defense of faith against those who attack it.

The word is derived from the Greek *apologia*, which means "defense." Apologists do not apologize for faith, regretfully acknowledging its fault or failure; rather, they speak a good word for God and attempt to vindicate faith by offering a defense of it against those who wish to demolish it. Apologetics states the case for belief and presents arguments to refute its assailants. Apologists offer apologetics without apology.

THEODICY: SPEAKING A GOOD WORD FOR GOD

When the apologists for faith put their minds to defending the goodness of God in the face of evil and suffering, what they produce is a theodicy. *Theodicy* is not a more sporting, slightly racier, and more appealing name for theology; it is an attempt to uphold and defend God and His ordering of the world in view of the existence of evil.

Defenders of faith come in all shapes and sizes, and their theodicies are as varied as they are. Some speak in the tight arguments and systematic discourse of philosophers and theologians while others spread themselves, finding more dramatic utterance in parables, plays, stories, and allegories. And one of them achieved sublime poetic expression in the greatest epic of our language. John Milton not only reasoned his theodicy into being but put it into verse and turned it into prayer, and told us exquisitely what it was he hoped to achieve with it:

> What in me is dark
> Illumine, what is low raise and support;
> That to the highth of this great argument
> I may assert eternal Providence,
> And justify the ways of God to men.

CHAPTER THREE

THE UNREASONABLENESS OF REASON

One reasonable objection to the very possibility of a reasoned defense of belief is the limitation of reason itself. It is not simply that we are not wise enough to solve the problem of evil, but that our reaction to it is often quickened by feeling rather than thought.

And so it should be. Life should not only be thought as clearly as we can ponder it, but felt as deeply as we can bear it. The difficulty is that our feelings are sometimes not thoughtful enough to be helpful, and may be passionate enough to be misleading.

This means that the shock of accident, the distress of natural disaster, the suffering of children, or the brutality of war may be so emotionally overwhelming as to numb the mind and threaten the thoughts, theories, and insights we had come to rely on to explain them. Our philosophy of suffering will often appear woefully inadequate in the face of suffering itself.

Patterns of understanding by which we interpreted the world's pain, and which seemed plausible enough when far enough removed from it, may be shaken by the immediacy of distress. The sight of one starving child is enough to scatter even our most profound arguments and leave us feeling trite and trivial.

THE WEAKEST FACULTY?

Jonathan Swift did not earn his university degree. The university finally gave it to him, embarrassed by the refusal of one of the most brilliant minds of his time to complete his studies under their discipline. Swift had refused to take the course in logic required for graduation, declaring, logically, that since our actions are not guided by logic, a course in the subject was unlikely to be of much use.

William James might have agreed with him. James considered reason the weakest of our faculties, being slave to our prejudices, susceptible to the fluctuations of our moods, and vulnerable to the volatility of our passions. Because of this, the coveted coolness and objectivity of reason are easily lost.

Reason is certainly at the mercy of our imagination. I discovered this when as a small child I was taken to hospital to have my tonsils out. The surgery required a general anesthetic, which was administered by putting a mask over my face and having me breathe chloroform. I knew I would not suffocate. My reason told me so. It was my mother who had brought me to the hospital, and she would sooner harm herself than hurt me. Yet rational conviction was useless against the sensation of smothering and the power of imagination. How I wanted to tear away the mask and escape!

"THE FOOL OF THE HOUSE"

This stranglehold of imagination on rational thought is confirmed for me every time I fly. As you know, flying is by far the safest way to travel. The statistics prove it beyond reasonable doubt. At the end of its flights Air Canada sometimes announces to the passengers as they prepare to get off the plane: "You are now beginning the most dangerous part of your journey. Please drive carefully."

Now, all this is well known to me; yet every time I enter the departure lounge at the airport I cast my eye over the other passengers and tell myself, "These are the people with whom you're going to die!" I have noticed that at thirty-three thousand feet statistics are no match for imagination. Saint Teresa did not know much about airplanes, but she knew enough about imagination to call it "the fool of the house."

STAYING POWER

We should remember, though, that while reason is often carried away by the power of our emotions, it has staying power. William James thought the staying power of reason one of its greatest and most helpful qualities. Anger, fear, sorrow, pity, disgust: these and other emotions can easily overwhelm us for a while, yet reason makes allowances for them, gives them room, outwaits them, and once more assumes its place of authority.

Once there, it affirms that while our emotions may bring home to us the inexpressible sadness of what we seek to explain, they do not necessarily alter the truth by which we attempt to explain it. Sensitivity of spirit will make us feel the pain of human distress more deeply; it need not disprove the insight by which we try to make sense of it. If my child were to be injured in an accident, my misery would be overwhelming; but it would not overthrow the principles by which I attempt to understand all accidents, though it might well heighten my sensibility in advancing them.

We can be of great assistance to those who are bewildered by loss, or distraught by grief, or overwhelmed by despair, by helping them to think dispassionately or by encouraging them to delay making important decisions until they are able to make them less emotionally and more rationally. For reason speaks to us, well, reasonably.

"In the Wee Small Hours"

Reason endures when passion has spent itself and prejudices have grown weary, for it knows enough not to stop. Moods change and emotions fade, but thought remains to steady and console us. It does so even in the wee small hours of the morning, which are so often the hour of the wolf and the dark night of the soul.

Nietzsche once complained that "when we are tired we are attacked by ideas we conquered long ago." Yet even when we are under attack because of weariness, our mind may still impart wise counsel by reminding us that "while sorrow endures for the night, joy comes with the morning." And with the dawn our thoughts will marshal themselves, and engage and conquer again the ideas they conquered long ago.

Indeed, our mind does more than that, for it acknowledges that our volatile emotions and fertile imaginations serve us well. Indignation, compassion, and fear are not only appropriate responses to some of the happenings of our days; they can give energy to our thought, quicken our imagination, and move us to action. Reason knows as it goes about its work that it is the work of the imagination to give it wings.

CHAPTER FOUR

QUESTIONABLE QUESTIONS

Another difficulty in dealing with the problem of evil is the impatience that sends us off in hot pursuit of an answer before we have properly understood the question. John Jay Chapman once remarked that there are plenty of people to whom the critical problems of their lives "never get presented in terms that they can understand." To those who demand instant explanations of profound matters, one is sometimes tempted to reply in the words of Jesus, "Ye know not what ye ask."

QUICK QUESTIONS

Time and again people come to me with what they call "a quick question," confident that their brief inquiry will require only an equally fast response. They are sometimes right. A short answer will occasionally suffice. But when it will not, the questioner may become impatient and wonder why his simple question cannot receive a simple reply. He may even suspect me of some sleight of mind by which I seek to evade his question by needlessly complicating my answer.

The difficulty is, of course, that a "simple" question may not be as simple as it sounds. In even the quickest query there may lurk ambiguity, equivocation, and confusion. We are very foolish indeed if we attempt to answer an inquiry we do not understand, or one that we suspect is confused in the mind of the person who makes it.

TRICK QUESTIONS

A good example of the devious nature of some questions is one question that was often the substance of a poor joke. "Tell me, have you stopped beating your wife?" the inquirer would ask, and smile at the struggles of the innocent as they attempted to answer it without getting themselves into trouble. Of course, the game is childish; yet even childish jokes may be instructive. If I were to answer that question by saying "Yes," then the questioner would be justified in thinking that I used to beat my wife but have abandoned the practice. And if I say "No," he will infer that I am still at it! No true "Yes or No" answer is possible, not because I am evasive, but because the questioner is mistaken in presuming that I ever did beat my wife. His question can be answered correctly only by first revealing his mistaken presumption. The truth of the matter is that I never did beat my wife and find it impossible to give up an activity in which I never engaged.

I have a friend who is among the great preachers in America. From time to time we have lunch together, and when we do he is apt to greet me by asking if I am still preaching his sermons. Now, how am I to answer the man? If I attempt a "Yes or No" answer, I am in the same difficulty as I have just described. "Yes" means I am still preaching his sermons, and "No" means that I once did but am no longer guilty of it.

The truth is that the questions we have considered are not really questions at all; they are disguised assertions. If they were meant seriously, they would be serious accusations. One asserts that we are wife-beaters, the other accuses us of plagiarism. The only way to "answer" them is to deny the presumptions that underlie them. This can have the double effect of resolving the ambiguity and spoiling the fun.

Yet it need not spoil the fun entirely. Last time my preacher friend accused me of preaching his sermons, I confessed that I had often thought of doing so but had not been able to find one I could deliver without wounding my reputation.

CONFUSING GOD'S WILL

The examples we have just tortured are puerile jokes; but think now of those wounded spirits who wish to know if their affliction is the will of God. How are we to answer them except by revealing the ambiguity of the phrase, "the will of God"? Do we mean by it what God intends should happen to them, or are we using the phrase in a much weaker sense to mean what God allows to happen to them without intending that it should? The first meaning may be the occasion of much spiritual anguish while the second may lead to renewed courage and deeper trust.

When I was teaching my little girl to walk, I did not intend that she should fall, bump her head, or bruise her knees; yet I allowed her to stumble and to sustain minor injuries because I intended that she should walk. I permitted her to fall, without intending that she should, in order to accomplish my real and happy intention.

"SORRY FOR YOUR TROUBLE"

One of the first funerals I ever conducted was of a baby girl who died of whooping cough. Shy neighbors gathered round the parents in their Fermanagh farmhouse, feeling awkward and inadequate and vaguely embarrassed in the presence of so grievous a loss, scarcely knowing what to say to bring the father and mother a bit of comfort. They all whispered, "I'm sorry for your trouble," and some added, "It's God's will."

Now, what did they mean by saying that the death of their neighbor's child was the will of God? Did they mean that God intended the tragedy, that He deliberately singled out this little family and sent this appalling sorrow to afflict them? But that would be a very wicked intention indeed, and we cannot make sense of it. If the doctor had been able to save the little one, would he thereby have foiled the divine intention? But if that is the case, then physicians frustrate the divine purpose a million times a day; and Jesus did, too, as He "went about doing good and healing all manner of disease."

"NOT SINGLE SPIES, BUT IN BATTALIONS"

Yet there is another possibility. When the farmers and their wives said, "It's God's will," perhaps they meant that though God did not deliberately choose and willfully intend that this little one should die, He nevertheless allowed her to. Her death, then, was the will of God in the sense that He permitted it to happen without intending that it should. Now if that is what they meant, then they were obviously correct; for we live in the sort of world where such tragedies are a daily occurrence, where troubles, when they come, may "come not single spies, but in battalions."

But again, those wise Fermanagh folk may have meant something deeper even than that when they attributed the little one's death to the will of God. I think it was their way of saying that when God allows things to happen to us that He does not intend should happen to us, we must not conclude that He doesn't care what happens to us. "The will of God" in this sense means that our distress does not carry us beyond God's care. When I allowed my little girl to stumble and fall while learning to walk, her bumps were not signs of her father's carelessness, but of his care.

"ONCE YOU SEE IT"

Dr. Leslie Weatherhead was one of the first to distinguish between what God intends, what He allows, and what He finally accomplishes. These are easy distinctions, once you think of them or once someone else thinks of them and tells you about them. Yet they are invaluable, not only in helping us to understand the will of God, but in flagging the ambiguity of much of our speech and many of our questions.

We shall return later to all of the issues raised in our discussion of the will of God, for we have raised them without resolving them. What we have tried to do in the last few paragraphs is to show how many different meanings may lurk in one short phrase of four short words, containing a total of only a dozen letters. This ambiguity must be spelled out before we can understand not only the answers we give but the questions we ask.

CHAPTER FIVE

O N D O I N G
T H I N G S
P E R F E C T L Y

TAKING ONE'S OWN MEDICINE

Suppose we were to take some of the ideas presented in the last chapter and apply them to the title of our book. What would we have to say about it in order to spell out any ambiguities that might be hidden there? We want to know why God doesn't do things perfectly, but that question raises half a dozen others before we have finished asking it.

For one thing, we should be able to say what these things are that God fails to do perfectly; and it would certainly be helpful if we had a clear notion of what we mean by perfection. Why doesn't God do *what* things perfectly, and what would it mean for Him to bring them to flawless consummation?

Now we are beginning to find ourselves in deep water; for it is clear that any perfection we might hope to achieve will be shaped, and may well be determined, by the nature of what it is we should like to perfect. Some of these things might even have their own ideas about their own perfection. And wouldn't it be prudent on our part to have some notion of what it is God wishes to do before we accuse Him of not doing it ideally?

"O BRAVE NEW WORLD!"

When we complain that God does not do things perfectly, what we are really asking is why the world is the way it is and not something other and better than it is. How are we to answer such a question?

To begin, by noticing the oddness of it. This world is the only world I know; and knowing it, I know I could never have imagined it. I could not have imagined imagination. Having lived in this world, I still cannot imagine it; and I cannot imagine how I am to imagine a world that is not only other than this, but better than this. Can you?

Oscar Wilde used to say that a poet does not see things as they are; if he did, he would in that moment cease to be a poet. But neither do our scientists, and they tell us we shouldn't either. They are eager to point out that reality is not what it appears to be, and they then go on to speak of fantastic things: that matter is energy, that light is subject to gravity, that if we increase the speed of an object we reduce the passage of its time.

This world of ours, they tell us, is not only stranger than we suppose, it is stranger than we *can* suppose. Our difficulty is not simply that we could never have imagined this world, but that even while living in it we cannot imagine it. We do not know what it is that we could not have imagined!

I sometimes write a fictional autobiography telling the story of what would have happened to me if I had not left Ireland nearly forty years ago. I have no doubt that I should have become prime minister. Northern Ireland is a small country where they used to say that everybody knows somebody who knows the prime minister.

The truth is, of course, that the day after I didn't leave Ireland I could have been knocked down by a lorry, struck by a terrorist's bullet, or drowned while bathing. Once we leave what actually did happen we have no way of knowing what would have happened. We cannot reimagine our own life, yet confidently undertake to reimagine the universe, and imagine that we are capable of doing it in such a way as to improve it! Talk about fools rushing in!

"Such People In'T"

But we have a further difficulty: how am I to know that in a perfect world there would be any place for me?

> O brave new world,
> That has such people in't!

Are all "such people" perfect?

Our present imperfect world, for all its limitations, has nevertheless produced us, with all our imperfections. This is, no doubt, an imperfect thing; but, as we have already seen, we cannot think it a regrettable thing. Would there be any place for imperfect people in this perfect world? We find ourselves sharing the dilemma of those who complain of the church's imperfections, forgetting that if the church were perfect it wouldn't let them in.

And what will happen to the imperfections of character that are the stuff of drama? If an imperfect Othello had not been so perfectly jealous he would, no doubt, have been a better man; but Shakespeare's play would not have been written, and Verdi's opera would never have been composed.

I have no doubt that dear Faustus, Doctor of Divinity, should not have been guilty of overreaching; yet if he had kept within safe limits we should never have known "the face that launched a thousand ships and burnt the topless towers of Ilium." Lady Macbeth is by any reckoning a nasty piece of work; but she is the power of a great play, and I am loathe to lose her. If only Hamlet could have made up his mind, and acted upon his resolve, his life, without a doubt, would have been much tidier; but it would also have been infinitely duller, and the chances are we should never have heard of him.

Lear's Lost Childhood

Someone suggested recently that psychoanalysis is a good way to talk about art and went on to say that if Lear's childhood had been happier, and if he had known himself loved for himself alone, and if one or two of his associates had read Freud and had treated their king with informed sensitivity, then the foolish, fond old man might not have gone mad. But then there would not be a play, either; and a world without the Prince of Denmark and King Lear is a more trivial, less splendid world. When we have made our world perfect will anyone ever exclaim, as Polly did in *Under Milk Wood,* "Oh, isn't life a terrible thing, thank God!"?

Here is another difficulty: how are we to reconcile what we might call "conflicting perfections"? What suits you perfectly may not suit me at all, and your ambitions may be at odds with my aspirations. If the consummation of your impeccable purpose frustrates my flawless intention, how will the matter be resolved? What are we to do when enterprises are incompatible and objectives clash?

It may be, of course, that in our brave new world tensions and conflicts of the sort we have described will be but "old, unhappy, far-off things, and battles long ago." But if so, what will have made them so? How are we to become, and who or what will make us, so perfect?

Puppets and Persons

When I first saw Walt Disney's *Pinocchio,* it came near to breaking my heart. Who could ever forget the magical moment when Gepetto, having wished upon a star, is granted the desire of his heart and his favorite puppet becomes his boy?

But Gepetto soon discovers that perfection in a puppet is not the same as perfection in a child. Pinocchio does not behave well with no strings attached. Before he has quite finished telling us that there are no strings to hold him down, he is off to town in the worst of company with a nose that grows longer by the minute from all the lies he tells.

I know an artist whose works are so splendid that if I were to call them masterpieces I should be stretching the word only a little. But the artist has discovered that while it may be difficult to paint a great picture, it is harder still to produce a wise, considerate, and mature son. You may think this comment unkind. You may think it unfair. You may rush to the father's defense and remind me that great characters and great canvases are not the same thing and cannot be produced in the same way. Indeed, you will want me to know that people are not "produced" at all; they are created or, rather, they create themselves; for they have hearts and minds and wills of their own and are not to be managed by anyone else. Magicians may be able to pull rabbits from hats by knowing and repeating the magic words, but there is no magic formula for the production of persons.

Which leads to another query: will this world of our dreaming be *completely* perfect? That is, will all the symphonies have been already composed, all the books written, and all the prose turned into poetry? Will the world be so perfectly finished that there will be no place in it for any imagination, creativity, invention of our own? Will God have already written a perfect book of the sort I am now attempting to write? Will all discoveries have been discovered? In short, will there be anything left for us to *do?*

HAVING WORDS WITH THE PSALMIST

The psalmist thought he could make the world more morally perfect by having God order it to better suit his expectations. What were his expectations? Well, they changed as one after the other was disappointed.

They started with the hope of special privileges for the righteous. A little more prosperity here, a little extra protection there, as a kind of faith-bonus would go far in winning friends for virtue.

When the special favors didn't materialize, the psalmist was prepared to settle for simple justice. It would suffice if God would reward the good and punish the wicked. That seemed only fair. But that didn't happen either. The good were not any better off than the bad. It was very disappointing and really discouraging.

But worse was to follow, for the wicked prospered. The bad people received the not-so-little extras the psalmist had coveted for the righteous. It was all too difficult to work out. Some of the good people were beginning to wonder whose side God was on. Why couldn't He do things right?

The psalmist asked his questions not only for himself, but for us; and what are we to make of them? Would the world be a more moral place if God were to accept the psalmist's suggestions, and ours?

Well, do we believe that God should have favorites? Would we think more highly of Him if He did? Or is it better that He should love all His children and make His sun to shine on the just and the unjust and His rain to fall on good and bad alike? Or should we wish to see the good rewarded and the wicked punished? It sounds just, yet it would not make the world more moral, but more morally ambiguous. If honesty is always the best policy, I will not know if you are truly honest or merely shrewd. If advancement comes to the good and affliction to the wicked, then who wouldn't be "good"?

And besides, we should be careful about asking for justice, because we cannot live by it. We do not live by justice, but by grace, mercy, and forgiveness. If justice means getting no more than we deserve, then who would wish for it? The psalmist complained that if God really loved us He would arrange His world differently. I want to say that it is because He loves us that He orders it the way He does.

In Robert Bolt's play, *A Man for All Seasons,* Sir Thomas More is visited in prison by his daughter Margaret. She argues like the psalmist until Sir Thomas tells her that if they lived in a state where virtue was profitable, then common sense would make us good and greed would make us saintly. Think once more of how the complaint of Margaret and the psalmist would work itself out. Suppose we knew that if we were kind we should never become ill, then everyone would be "kind" so as to avoid sickness. But to be kind is to act, not for reasons of self-interest, but to help others. Kindness means acting for their sakes, not our own. To take Margaret or the psalmist's advice, then, would be to destroy kindness itself. The psalmist and Margaret's suggestion would not make the world more moral. It would make disinterested goodness difficult to achieve and impossible to identify.

GOOD TASTE AND THINGS THAT TASTE GOOD

Once again, how can we be sure that any world we might be able to think of will be perfect? Goethe warns us of the mischief done by people who have imagination and no taste. In designing our new world, then, whose taste should we rely on? Just the other day I saw a man driving a purple car, and the day before that I spotted a woman in a pink one. Should they be entrusted with the choice of, say, the new world's colors? Now, my own refinement is more refined than theirs and improving all the time. How long should I wait, then, before trusting my taste by committing myself to particular ideas of shape, hue, quality, and material? I am embarrassed at present to remember the things I thought tasteful just ten years ago. Five years from now I might be appalled to behold what I could cheerfully choose tomorrow. My idea of perfection is changing all the time, and I know I should be able to design a prettier world twelve months from now than I could manage at the moment.

ON NOT LEAVING IT TO THE EXPERTS

Might it not be safer, then, to hand the whole thing over to the experts and perfectionists and allow them to conceive it? Yet experts are often less than competent (the taps in my bathroom cannot be turned off with wet hands), and perfectionists are, for the most part, insufferable. (One of the most endearing things about God is that He is not a perfectionist.)

Choosing materials will not be easy, for it will not mean merely choosing one kind of stuff rather than another, but making up our minds if it should be a material world at all. Would it not be better to dispense with the physical: with bodies, things, matter, stuff, and substance, with all their attendant aches, pains, wear, and decay? This would mean, of course, an end to food and flavors, sights and sounds, fragrances and sensations. It is hard to imagine how there could be any sex in such a world, or how children could continue to be *loved* into existence; and, if they are, will it be possible to invent a love that is pain-free, in roughly the same way we have invented the fat-free cookies and sugar-free candies that manage to be almost flavor-free?

I fear I am beginning to sound, and I know I am beginning to feel, a little giddy trying to imagine this new world; and my proposals are getting out of control and are carrying me far beyond my own good sense. I am not sure how to get out of it or how to go on with it. Which is exactly how Augustine began to feel when his few suggested improvements to the world he knew brought him to the brink of absurdity, so that he drew back in astonishment and humility. He was out of his depth, and was bright enough to know it. Yet we may share, not only his discomfort, but his conclusion:

> I no longer wished for a better world because I was thinking of the whole creation, and in the light of this clearer discernment I have come to see that though the higher things are better than the lower, the sum of all creation is better than the higher things alone.

We are told that when Job complained about the state of his world, God answered him out of the whirlwind. The interesting thing is that God's answer to Job was a question, or a series of questions, so that the questioner found himself questioned.

The questions are simple and may not seem like much of an answer to a man who has just lost his family to violent death. One of them, for example, wants to know if Job has considered the crocodile. There follows a description of the crocodile that is precise in its observation and eloquent in its appreciation. It is really a way of asking whether Job has learned to appreciate the wonder of the world he lives in before complaining about it and trying to imagine a better one.

CHAPTER SIX

THE POWER AND PURPOSE OF GOD

EITHER/OR

e gave the problem of evil a particular expression when we made it into a question by asking why God does not do things perfectly. We then went on to pose it in a rather different way by asking why the world is what it is and not something else. By "something else" we meant not only something different, but something better. If God wants a perfect world, why does He not make it so? What's holding Him back? Is He not able to produce it?

We must now notice the most common form in which the problem of evil has been stated. It asserts that God is either all-good but not all-powerful, or else He is all-powerful but not all-good. Evil exists because God either cannot or will not do anything about it.

Let me put that in other words so that we can catch the flavor of it. God either wants to do things perfectly, but cannot; or He could do things perfectly but will not. He either has the will but lacks the ability, or He has the ability but lacks the will. Either He has good intentions that He can't pull off, or He lacks the good intentions He could pull off if He only had them. He is deficient in either power or goodness. Here is how David Hume put it:

> Is God willing to prevent evil, but not able?
> Then He is impotent.
> Is He able, but not willing?
> Then is He malevolent.

IMPOTENT OR MALEVOLENT?

When the problem of evil is put in this way, it not only gives us a clear choice, but gets rid of the problem however we choose. It explains the presence of evil in the world by saying that God either cannot or will not get rid of it. Either way, the reality of evil, the sheer brute fact of it, is untouched; but the problem of why it exists is solved. It exists because God is either impotent or malevolent. The choice may be a clear one, but it is not a happy one for believers. The difficulty with this either/or answer to the question of evil is that either/or always wipes something out. We forfeit either one side or the other. Something has to go, and what goes in this instance is one of God's fundamental attributes. God is diminished however we choose, for He is stripped either of His power or of His goodness.

ABLE OR WILLING?

Whichever way we choose, then, will mean the death of God. For what kind of God is He who is good but has no power, and who will believe in Him? Or what kind of God is He who has power but is not good, and who will trust Him? We have solved the problem of evil by getting rid of God.

It should be no surprise that believers are unwilling to do so. They wish to affirm both the power and the goodness of God, for that is what it means to be a believer. When they gather for worship they "tell of His might [and] sing of His grace" and call to each other from every part of their house of worship to every other part of it:

> O worship the King,
> All-glorious above;

> O gratefully sing
> His power and His love.

They are suspicious of any account of evil that explains its presence by dismissing God from the world. They think that Hume's way of stating the reason for the existence of evil is too cut and dried, a little too clever, a shade too neat and tidy, and a fraction too final and confident. They imagine that there might be more going on in it than meets the eye, so they will persist in believing in God and will allow the puzzle of evil to linger a while unsolved, just to see what they can do with it. Indeed, Hume offers them this choice in his third and fourth questions about God and His ability or willingness to deal with the ills that afflict us:

> Is He both able and willing?
> Whence then is evil?

THE NATURE OF POWER

The classic statement of the enigma of evil is that it is in the world because God lacks either the power or the will to get rid of it. But what do we mean when we speak of God's power, and how is it related to His goodness, or will, or purpose? Perhaps if we were to better understand the nature of God's power and how it is directed by His intention, we might discover how it is that evil can exist, even though God is both omnipotent and good.

Our first thought of omnipotence takes it to mean that God can do anything and everything. It is obvious that to have power is to be able to do things, and the more power we have the more things we are able to do. To possess ultimate power, or omnipotence, is to be able to do everything. With omnipotence, anything goes, for nothing is beyond its capacity. There are no limits to omnipotence.

CAPABLE OF ANYTHING?

Now, this is our first thought about the nature of omnipotence, and it is an excellent reason why we should have second thoughts about it. And the first question our second thought asks is whether being able to do anything means being able to do something we do not wish to do. If it does mean that, then it is very odd indeed; for our common sense tells us that if we do something we have no wish to do, then what we possess is not power, but weakness.

It would seem, then, that as soon as we begin to think about it, our understanding of power must be modified to mean, not the ability to do anything, but the capability to accomplish anything we wish to accomplish. This means that it is useless to speak of power or ability without relating it to our intention or purpose.

This moves us a giant step forward in our understanding of power; for what are wishes but the expression of the self, its values, priorities, desires, ambitions, and hopes? In short, our wishes reveal our character, and are an expression of it. If you thought me capable of anything, you would not consider me omnipotent, you would take me for a rogue; as the Irish say, "You wouldn't trust me as far as you could throw me." And you would be right. If we are capable of anything, we have no honor. If there isn't anything we wouldn't do, we have no character.

THE CHARACTER OF OMNIPOTENCE

When we speak of the divine omnipotence, then, we cannot mean by it that God is capable of anything, or that there isn't anything He wouldn't do. If that is what we mean, then our description of omnipotence fits the devil far better than it describes God. If God is capable of anything, He has no character and His power is not anything we should praise. If His omnipotence is not the expression of His goodness, then it is to be dreaded, and not worshiped.

When we realize this, we begin to understand why the classic statement of the problem of evil is simplistic and inadequate. It assumes that God's omnipotence means He is capable of doing anything, even things that are not consistent with either His nature or His purpose. Before we say that God is either impotent or malevolent because of his failure to do what we think He should do, perhaps we ought to ask what it is that God wishes to do, and how His power expresses His character and His intention.

"MAY GOD STRIKE ME DEAD!"

What we have been saying is well illustrated by the old story of the atheist who was determined to demonstrate once and for all that God does not exist. He struck a match in a public place and called upon God, if He existed, to prove His existence to all the spectators by striking him dead before the match went out. When the flame died away, and the man did not, any hope of his ever believing in God died with it.

We think the story a little silly, yet it is not very different from the argument of David Hume; and for that reason it is worth looking at for a moment to notice just where it goes wrong. In our anecdote, the confident atheist concluded that because the Almighty did not strike him dead when challenged to do so, God does not exist. But there are other ways to explain the man's survival.

It may be, for example, that God does exist but has no wish to play silly games with foolish atheists, or by their rules. Or God may think He is under no obligation to react just because those who do not believe in Him decide to put Him to the test. Or again, it may not be part of the divine nature to wipe people out even when they are silly enough to invite Him to. Indeed, it might be that the divine refusal to do so is a demonstration, not of His nonexistence, but of His patience and mercy and divine sense of humor. It may even be that God has other plans for the atheist because He loves him and is not yet through with him. It is one of God's little jokes that atheists like Jean Paul Sartre, for example, who spend their time denying that He exists, somehow cannot get Him out of their minds. And haven't some one-time agnostics become first-rate apologists?

THE ABILITY TO ACHIEVE PURPOSE

This brings us very close indeed to a definition of power, so I am going to risk one by saying that power is the ability to achieve purpose; it is the competence to accomplish whatever it is we wish to accomplish. And because wishes and purposes are expressions of the self, and are thus the vital part of character, power is not merely what we have the means to accomplish, but what our character will allow us to accomplish.

We must be clear that the kind of definition we have offered is not a limitation of power; or at least, it is not the sort of limitation we should ever wish to object to. Nor does it present us with a limited God. To be able to express our nature by accomplishing what we purpose to accomplish is not only an expression of power, but its fulfillment.

There is an enlightening story told of a Scottish Covenanter charged with treason and hauled before an English king for judgment. The king asked him imperiously, "Do you know that it is within my power to release you?" To which the canny Scot, who already counted himself a dead man, replied, "Your Majesty, it may be within your power, but it's no' within your nature!"

There are many things that are not within our power because they are not within our nature. If you will forgive an Irish way of putting it, there are many things we could do, except that we couldn't do them! I am physically strong enough to injure a little child, yet the very thought of it is abhorrent to me. To use my power in that way would be to offend every value I cherish and every ideal I honor. As we say, it isn't in me to do it; and that inability is not a limitation of my power but an expression of my nature.

THE WEAKNESS OF GOD

If power is the ability to achieve purpose, then we should not be surprised if there are times when it looks like weakness. What we sometimes need if we are to accomplish our purpose is not noise, forcefulness, and might, but gentleness, patience, and restraint. Yet these qualities are often taken to be signs of weakness, not expressions of power. Yet physical strength, moral influence, intellectual superiority, however impressive they may appear, are not power if they do not achieve what we wish to accomplish by them.

I knew a man once who didn't like his daughter's boyfriend and decided one evening to put on a show of force to show his disapproval. He was full of sound and fury. He screamed at the girl, banged on the table, and threw the furniture about, withering the plants and terrifying the dog and the goldfish. "Don't you see that young man again!" he commanded. He was clear, decisive, imperious, dominant. And when he had finished, his daughter rose, put on her coat, gathered a few of her things, and moved into her boyfriend's apartment.

"THE SILENT MOVER"

Set beside this demonstration of weakness the power of James Reston, former executive editor of *The New York Times*, and thought by some to be the most influential journalist of his generation. Mr. Reston was a great admirer of Jean Monet, the

French visionary, and loved to quote and put into practice one of his sayings, "If you don't demand credit for things, you can push them through." There were times when James Reston was perfectly content to stay invisible, to be "the silent mover of the play" and remain unacknowledged, so long as he achieved his purpose.

When David Hume charges God with impotence for not banishing evil from the world, it may just be that the philosopher has not given enough consideration to what it is God wants to do with His world and those who dwell in it. Perhaps what Hume calls God's impotence is God's way of doing what it is He wishes to achieve. Maybe James Reston is a better clue to God's style than either the philosopher or the man who threw the furniture about.

Indeed, we should have no doubt of the truth of this, for we see it in all God's dealings with His children. It is there that the nature of His power is truly revealed. What God wishes to accomplish in His children is to charm their fears, awaken their trust, sustain their freedom, quicken their faith, secure their honor, kindle their hope, and woo and win their love. Such ends cannot be brought about by force or accomplished by coercion. The power that achieves them will be of a gentler sort.

MOBY DICK AND SILENT NIGHT

What are we to make of it, then, when the Christmas choirs burst into the "Hallelujah!" chorus, proclaiming with heart and voice and every kind of instrument that "the Lord God Omnipotent reigneth"? What sort of omnipotence is this, and how will it be brought to bear on us? The same voices give us the answer when they sing:

> Unto us a Child is born,
> Unto us a Son is given.

This is how God's omnipotence is brought to bear on human pride, folly, wickedness, and estrangement; for God's way of dealing with evil is to overcome it with good. He gets rid of His enemies by making them His friends.

For what are we to do with an Omnipotence that not only holds the world in its hands, but lays itself in a mother's arms; that refuses to negotiate except from weakness; that is so afraid of being overbearing that we sometimes cannot even find it; that so disguises itself that we fail to recognize it, and call it by other and lesser names; that refuses to put its signature on anything and is heard, not in the thunder, the earthquake, or the fire, but in "a sound of gentle stillness," a baby's whimper, and a young man's cry of Godforsakenness?

No one saw this more clearly or expressed it more eloquently than Herman Melville. When *Pequod* is caught in a violent storm, and is illumined from bow to stern in a supernatural light, Captain Ahab screams his hostility to overwhelming omnipotence and his hospitality to power of another sort:

> I know Thee, Thou clear Spirit, and I know that Thy proper worship is defiance! Come to me as Power and there is that here which to the last gasp of this earthquake life will resist Thee. But come in Thy lowest form of love, and I will kneel and kiss Thee.

What Hume called impotence is what some have called the foolishness of God and the weakness of God. But to those who believe, it is the Power of God and the Wisdom of God. What Hume called impotence, Christians call grace. It is "Thy lowest form of love," an Omnipotence we may worship with a kiss.

CHAPTER SEVEN

THE NATURE OF EVIL

We have noticed that one of the reasons why God looks impotent has to do with the nature of what it is He wishes to accomplish in His children. Our difficulty is that we are tempted to think that the Divine intention should correspond to our all-too-human expectation; and when it does not, we think God inept for not doing what we think He ought to do. We wonder why He doesn't give us a more attentive hearing and adopt our suggestions when we have gone to all the trouble to list them, not just alphabetically, but in order of importance.

The answer is that God has ends and purposes of His own which are better than ours: both more loving and more subtle. We expect Him to use His power to do what we think He should do, and by His power we mean sheer force. But we cannot bully people into loving us, and we cannot force them into trusting us. That sort of power doesn't work even in human relationships, and to expect God to behave in ways that are both offensive to us and useless in accomplishing His ends is conceited and silly. We presume to instruct God with the kind of advice we would not, or should not, offer a fellow-mortal.

"YOU MADE ME LOVE YOU"

A man came to me once in great distress because his wife had become unhappy enough with him to move out of the house. She said she needed a little space in which to possess herself and assess their relationship before deciding what she should do next.

What had bothered her most about her husband was his cold presumptuousness, his domineering spirit, and lack of consideration. He often made important decisions that affected both of them without even mentioning them to her. Her own proper sense of self could no longer tolerate what she considered a serious failure of love and respect on his part.

Now that she had left, her husband wanted to know from me what it was he should do to get her back. I said I thought it was not merely a time for him to think of how he might win her back, but to give some serious thought to the nature of their relationship, and especially to his own behavior. I thought he should begin by showing her that he cared for her enough to respect her wish for a little space. He should reassure her, not by promising to do better, but by demonstrating in the present circumstances that he was doing better already. He now had an opportunity to show his wife a spirit of respect, gentleness, and consideration. He should win her again by kindness. And his kindness should not be a mere tactic or stratagem, but a true expression of his thoughtfulness, patience, and affection.

He agreed with me, and said he would do it; but he didn't. He pursued her with the same aggressiveness and insensitivity that had driven her away in the first place. He demonstrated by his every action that if she returned to him, nothing would have changed. What would be waiting for her was what she had left. Every attempt to pressure her into coming back to him, whether by tears of self-pity or by unrestrained anger, served only to confirm the rightness of her decision to leave. She never returned.

When we sing, "You made me love you," the "making" is not a bullying, but a winning. If God sometimes looks inept it is because He will make us love Him, not by terror, but by tenderness.

FINDING THE RIGHT METAPHOR

But there is another reason why God may sometimes look either impotent or malevolent in His relation to the existence of evil, and it has to do with the nature of evil itself. When we wonder why God doesn't get rid of the evils in the world, the image we have is of clearing out the closets or putting out the garbage. We think that evils should be singled out, picked up, and thrown away. Or we wonder why God does not zap them with supernatural energy, or by divine fiat command them to be off.

An even more telling metaphor is to think of evil as a thorn in our pet's paw. We would not waste a moment in taking it out and restoring the poor creature to comfort and mobility. Or we remember the bad tooth that once afflicted us with much pain until it was extracted to our immediate and enormous relief. And that, we think, is how God should deal with the ills that afflict. He should pull them out to the relief of all who suffer.

It sounds simple, but its simplicity is spurious. There would be nothing wrong with the metaphors if evils really were like poisonous thorns or any other sort of discrete entity that we could get our hands on to extract and discard. But they are not. Evils are not things at all. We cannot grab a handful of them or gather them up and put them in a box or plastic bag and set them out to be picked up and taken away. They are nothing of a sort that we could point to or put our hands on. We could not frisk an evil man and find them or search his home and confiscate them.

Evils are not extraneous entities; they are not entities at all. You cannot separate the evil of an evil man from the man himself, for it is an expression of his nature. Evil is not a broken headlight on my car, easily smashed and almost as easily replaced; it is not even a dent in the fender of my car; it is a pervasive and corroding rust that has weakened the integrity of its frame, and neither slumbers nor sleeps as it continues to consume the vehicle.

If we are to think of evils as physical ailments—and it is a useful way for us to think of them, for they are certainly not healthy—then they are not a wound inflicted from without, but cancers that grow from within. Evil is leukemia, not a thorn in the flesh or a sore tooth. The trouble with it is that it is a disease, not of our bad cells, but of our good cells out of control. The great difficulty in treating many forms of cancer is that it is hard to be rid of the unhealthy cells without destroying the healthy ones. As one specialist working in cancer research said to me recently, when we are dealing with cancer it is not merely to learn the nature of an illness, but to discover the structure of life itself.

GOOD EGGS AND BAD APPLES

Augustine makes this truth basic to his theodicy. Evils are not things in themselves, but are good things gone wrong. They have no self-sufficient, independent existence, but are parasites that cannot exist apart from the life and being of the goodness that is their host. This is how he put it:

> Things solely good can, in some circumstances, exist; things solely evil, never; for even those natures which are vitiated by an evil will, so far indeed as they are vitiated are evil, but insofar as they are natures they are good.

We may discover this in a number of ways. One is that when we identify something we simply say what it is. An egg is an egg. What we call a good egg is just an egg. But when we speak of a bad egg we are not naming another sort of thing, we are describing the same sort of thing gone bad. An apple is an apple. When we name it we name a fruit of a particular kind.

But a bad apple is not another kind of fruit, it is the same sort of fruit gone rotten. I might even risk a pun and say that it is a fallen apple.

In a similar way, lies do not exist in themselves, but only in relation to the truth they falsify. The existence of lies always presumes the existence of truth. Lies are not only false, they are unnatural. To tell lies successfully requires a good memory, but not so the telling of truth. To speak the truth is to speak naturally, without division in ourselves or dissimulation towards others; and we do not need to remember what we said last time in order to tell the same story this time.

Our everyday vocabulary gives us another hint of the derivative nature of evils when we remember that many of the words we use to describe what is not pleasing to us are words that simply undo, or negate, the words that describe what is pleasing to us. We just put *un-* or *dis-* or *in-* in front of them to express how we feel or tell what we suffer. Joy is happiness, and to be miserable is to be un-happy; constancy is faithfulness, to be in-constant is to be un-faithful; health is ease and sickness is dis-ease; to be content is to be satisfied, while to be restless is to be dis-satisfied, or dis-contented.

Evils are not things in themselves; we define them as negations of the qualities, virtues, attitudes, and emotions we experience as positive goods. We literally cannot speak of corruption, perversion, or degradation without declaring in each of the words we choose the prior reality of the good that has been corrupted, perverted, degraded, or spoiled in some other way.

A WARNING AGAINST WEEDING

Jesus made the inseparability of good and evil plain in the profound story that is best known as the parable of the wheat and the tares. It tells of a farmer who sowed wheat in his fields and of an enemy who, wishing to work some mischief, sowed darnel among the wheat during the hours of darkness. When the wheat and the weeds had sprouted enough for the farmer's men to discover this, they wanted to know if they should pull up the darnel. The farmer replied that if they attempted to do so they would risk rooting out the wheat along with the weeds. Not only did the wheat and the darnel look alike, their roots would have intertwined to such an extent as to be inseparable. To pull up one would be to pull up the other. They should be allowed to grow together until harvest, when they could be more easily separated.

I have a friend who nurtures plants in pots in her office. One of them has been joined by a weed of undiscoverable pedigree which takes its share of the nourishment intended for the flowers. But my friend is reluctant to pull it out, for who knows what intertwining of roots has gone on in the deep soil of the pot? She may not approve of the weed, but the primula may have grown fond enough of it to have formed a serious attachment. Separation might prove traumatic.

GIFTS AND LIMITATIONS

We have learned the truth of this from our own awareness of ourselves. We know that our limitations are often the other side of our qualities, and our failings a twisting of our gifts. Our fears are inseparable from our imagination, and our anxiety from our creativity. Our love of excellence may make us inordinately critical, and our ambition may render us ruthless. If we are highly intelligent we may be unable to suffer fools gladly, and our enthusiasms may make us insensitive. We know that some of our worst blunders should be attributed, not to our wickedness, but to our abilities, aptitudes, and gifts carrying us too far, too fast, with too little restraint or awareness.

Reinhold Niebuhr used to say that pretension is the sin of all good people. Pretension is undoubtedly sinful, for it is not only self-aggrandizement, but self-deceit. Yet it is not a thing in itself, but a distortion of goodness. Self-righteousness is a wicked attitude, but it would be impossible without respect for what is right and a care for virtue. Many of the evils that spoil our character and afflict our society are not things evil in themselves, but good qualities that are out of control.

Chesterton once said that part of the trouble with our world is that the old Christian virtues have gone mad, have separated themselves, and are now wandering about on their own. They have thereby lost their ability to modify, restrain, and protect each other. We all know people who care only for truth, and so have become pitiless; and we are aware of others who care only for pity, and so have become untruthful. We know that courage is not only a quality important in itself, but one that is essential to sustain many other virtues, including love; yet if courage lacks the restraint and instruction of wisdom it may become impulsive and foolish, and prove more harmful than timidity. Reinhold Niebuhr gave us a truth to live by, one that can save us from cynicism and despair, when he said that much evil is done, not by evil men, but by good men who lack knowledge.

THE PRIORITY OF GOODNESS

We may learn at least two important lessons from this. The first is that while it seems a simple complaint to ask why God does not rid the world of evil, and to charge Him with impotence for not doing so, the complaint is not as simple as it sounds. If evils are essentially good things gone wrong, how are we to be rid of them without threatening the very goodness apart from which they would not exist? The second lesson is to recognize the priority of goodness.

By the priority of goodness we mean that goods and evils do not coexist as equals; one is prior to the other in such a way that the other cannot exist without it. Good can exist without evil; but evil cannot exist without the good of which it is a distortion or negation. Lies presuppose that there is such a thing as truth, for they could not come to be without it, and they have no life save in the falsifying of it. But truth can exist without lies, for it is a positive good and has existence in itself.

DR. JEKYLL AND MR. HYDE

Chesterton put this, not only plainly, but personally, when he came to comment on what he considered a common misunderstanding of Stevenson's *Dr. Jekyll and Mr. Hyde.* The story is frequently taken to mean that a man can cut himself off from his conscience and may be cloven into two personalities, good and evil, which are considered to be equal, with neither caring for the other. Chesterton thought the meaning of the story quite different from that. It is that a man *cannot* cut himself off from his conscience, because while evil does not care for good, good must care about evil. Good is the God in man and insists on knowing the whole self. Evil is homeless and does not care for anything. Chesterton thought this good psychology, good theology, and the stuff of good storytelling. George Macdonald sums up Chesterton splendidly: "The darkness knows neither the light nor itself; only light knows itself and darkness also."

This priority of goodness explains how someone came to lament the scarcity of hypocrites. He meant by his complaint that it is impossible to be hypocritical without admitting to some norm of virtue which the hypocrite will at least pretend to have attained. More hypocrites would mean a wider acknowledgment of some moral standard that would be perversely honored by their false claim to have achieved it. That is why a seventeenth-century Frenchman called hypocrisy the homage vice pays to virtue.

"The Only Hopeful Doctrine"

It is important to notice that what we have said about the nature of evils, that they are not existences in themselves, but good things gone wrong, makes a statement, not only about the nature of evil, but about the nature of the world. What it says is that this is not an evil world, but a good world gone wrong. This is one of the great truths declared in the magnificent myth of the Fall. Everytime we repeat the Genesis story, we affirm that this world of ours is not evil, but fallen; as Chesterton once put it, we are not entrapped in a bad world but have misused a good one. To Chesterton this meant that the Fall is not merely one view of life; it is the only enlightening and encouraging view of life. The world is Paradise Lost, for there is nothing in it that is as it should be. Yet a Paradise Lost holds out some hope of a Paradise Regained, in which all things might attain fullness of being.

One of the reasons we believe in God at all is that in this world we are haunted by the sense of a lost perfection and mourn for a lost good. If we have never been able to consider ourselves more than strangers and pilgrims on the earth, it suggests there may be another world that is our true home. The warped goodness, bent virtue, and broken beauty that are the best we know in this world point us beyond its imperfections to a Transcendent Loveliness, to what Plotinus called "The Beauty Yonder," in which our inconsolable longings find not only their consolation but their fulfillment. That is why our earthly journey may be aptly described as our pilgrimage from "The Land of Lost Content" to "The Land of Heart's Desire."

We cannot have a wholly evil world; for such a world could not exist, since existence is itself a good. We cannot even imagine it; for evil cannot be separated from the good of which it is the frustration, distortion, and denial. It is splendid and natural to think of God breaking the awful silence with the first words of Creation, "Let there be light!" but it is impossible to imagine Him saying, "Let there be darkness!" We should not know what darkness is if we had not first seen and known the light.

THE DEVIL CAN'T BE *THAT* BAD!

Notice, further, that it would be just as impossible to imagine a creature who was totally depraved as it would be to conceive of a world that was purely evil. We sometimes think that the Devil is such a being; for is he not the repository and distillation of every sort of corruption, degradation, and perversion?

Yet if the Devil were totally depraved, he could not know it; for the awareness of depravity is itself a moral insight. We say that the Devil is wholly evil, yet allow that he is resourceful and fully capable of acting resolutely and cunningly. Why, he possesses enough intelligence to outwit even the brightest among us and is more astute than we are. He knows us better than we understand ourselves and is bright enough, and wicked enough, to exploit, deceive, and destroy us by his malice.

We forget that in describing the Devil thus we have had to mention half a dozen qualities that are good in themselves, even though used to wicked ends and diverted to base purposes. You will remember that in his *Paradise Lost,* Milton had to endow Satan with enough power, fortitude, and resourcefulness to contend with God and keep the contest interesting.

When C. S. Lewis wrote his *Screwtape Letters,* he came to dislike the book intensely because to write it he had to get inside the brain of the wicked Wormwood and think like the Devil. But a Devil that thinks like Lewis can't be all bad. The evils in the world are not things in themselves to be independently accounted for by being attributed to a malevolent creative power; they are good things gone wrong.

"TRUMPETS IN THE MORNING"

This is the truth that is being affirmed when the Devil is described as a fallen angel. An old story tells us that when Satan, now reigning in hell, was asked what it was he missed most about his former celestial life, he replied, "The sound of trumpets in the morning!" Satan, too, is something or someone who was once good, but turned bad, and is still vulnerable to nostalgia! And that is why Jews, Christians, and Muslims are not dualists. We do not attempt to explain the world, or the good and evil in it, by attributing the good to one Creator and the evil to another. Satan is not another divinity of equal power and authority with the one true God who called the world into being from the goodness and love that He is. As Martin Luther once put it, Satan is always God's Satan.

We are monists, not dualists; for we believe that the world was created by one God. This is not only what we believe about God, it is how the world appears to us. Dualism is to be rejected because it corresponds neither to the nature of evils nor to the nature of the world. The evils in the world are not things in themselves to be accounted for by being attributed to a malevolent creative power; they are good things gone wrong. And the world itself is a good world fallen. And Satan fell.

But if that is the nature of evils, then it explains why it is so difficult even for God to be rid of them; for they cannot be separated from the good things to which they cling. To arbitrarily dispense with them would be like throwing out the baby with the bath water, and that would be an expression of neither wisdom nor power.

CHAPTER EIGHT

THE STUFF OF THE WORLD

TWO HEADS BETTER THAN ONE?

hen we have attributed the work of creation to the love and goodness of one Creator rather than to a struggle between two originators of different minds and natures, we have not solved the problem of evil; in a sense we have made it worse. The nature of the world becomes more baffling when we believe that God could get on with making it without any opposition from a powerful, supernatural rival. If He had things all His own way, then why are things the way they are? As Woody Allen would pose the question, "Is God an underachiever?"

We assume that, in deciding on the sort of world He was going to make, God considered His options, made up His mind, and then got on with it. Our question is why He decided to get on with what He got on with. If every possibility He considered was an out-of-this-world possibility, why did He make the imperfect world we know? Why, for example, did He choose to make it a physical and material world with its attendant shocks, accidents, privations, miseries, disasters, diseases, and death?

There is an important sense in which our question can make little sense and really is a dead end. God may know what His options were; but we do not, nor can we begin to imagine them. And even if we could, we have no way of knowing whether the kind of world we could imagine would have been possible even to omnipotence. The most we can hope is that this world of ours is the best of all possible worlds, not the best of all impossible ones.

CONSIDERING THE HIPPOPOTAMUS

All we can do, then, is assume that, whatever His options, God made the wisest and most loving choice when He created this round earth of ours and from its imagined corners brought us to life and being. We can attempt to understand the world and try to make sense of its fierce enigmas, especially those that are of such a nature as to make us question the wisdom and love of its Creator. It will surely be more helpful to consider the nature of the world God chose to make than spend our time and energy trying to explain any number of worlds that He might have made, but did not, and that are beyond our power to imagine.

We spoke of this earlier when we pointed out that it is easier to bring a complaint against an imperfect world than it is to imagine a perfect one. We should now remind ourselves that this imperfect world of ours not only affords us many reasons and much opportunity to complain about it, but also invites us to understand and appreciate it. In the language of the book of Job, it wants to know if we have considered the hippopotamus and the crocodile in order to gain what we can in appreciation and understanding.

WHAT'S THE MATTER WITH MATTER?

It seems a little odd, and not a little ungrateful, to ask why God made the world out of material stuff, and filled it from sky to ocean floor with physical creatures, without first acknowledging the marvel this world of matter is. There really isn't much the matter with matter; for it does any number of things very well indeed and is pliable and versatile enough to accommodate our own needs, desires, and aspirations.

We are tempted to think of matter as heavy, cloddish stuff—nothing if not coarse, crude, and indelicate. And there is no doubt that it was exactly that to begin with, for our creation began in an explosion of unimaginable magnitude and force. To say that we are made of stardust may sound poetic, but it is also a literal truth. Our world and everything in it is made of stardust, for our earth is a fragment of an exploded star.

When we say this, it should not be spoken to lament the crudeness of creation, but to marvel that what began so violently should have achieved the measure of refinement it now possesses. Indeed, the bounds of its sophistication are set, not by the limitations of matter, but by the limits of our imagination.

HYMN TO MATTER

God creates us, then, by first making everything in which our being is grounded, and He exploded a star to do it. To make us, God had to create a world in which our physical being is rooted and which is the stuff of our life. A couple I know announced the birth of their son by sending to their friends a card containing a question-and-answer verse by George Macdonald:

> Where did you come from, baby dear?
> Out of the Everywhere into the here.
> Where did you get your eyes so blue?
> Out of the sky as I came through.

Macdonald is exactly right. He puts the truth poetically, as poets do, but there are facts behind his every word. If there is no Everywhere, there can be no here. If there are no blue skies there will be no blue eyes, nor brown eyes either for that matter. If no stars twinkle, no eyes will shine; no galaxies, no gaiety; no Milky Way, no path for our feet. To make you and me God had

to put rain on the wind and cloud-shadows on the hills, cast
rainbows over the sun, and wash the world with moonbeams.
This claim is not peculiar to us. We make it, not for ourselves alone, but for all created things that cannot claim it for
themselves. Once again, the poets are onto it: Augustus
Bamberger makes it plain that what is true of us is just as true
of any tree, fruit, or flower:

> There's a part of the sun in an apple,
> There's a part of the moon in a rose,
> There's a part of the flaming Pleiades
> In every leaf that grows.

Maltbie Babcock shapes the same thought into a grace to grace
any table:

> Back of the loaf is the snowy flour,
> And back of the flour the mill;
> And back of the mill is the wheat and the shower,
> And the sun and the Father's will.

But it is Sidney Lysaght who tells it best of all in "The Valley
of Wild Thyme" when a child asks what it takes to make a rose
and receives the sublime answer:

> It takes the world's eternal wars;
> It takes the moon and all the stars;
> It takes the might of heaven and hell,
> And the Everlasting Love as well,
> Little child.

SIBELIUS AND STARDUST

In one way or another, everything in our world is the result
of a cosmic bang. Who could ever have imagined that from an
exploding star there could come all the loveliness we know?

Not long ago, I watched a violinist take a piece of wood with taut strings attached, tuck it under his chin, and scrape the strings using another piece of wood, bowed and with softer cords. And from those fragments of an exploded star he brought forth a melody that wrenched my heart. What an unimaginable journey from stardust to Sibelius!

There is, as we have said, no end to this exquisite refinement of matter; for the marvel was not just the violin, but the creativity of the composer, the sensitivity of the artist, and even these ears and this brain of mine that could pluck their music from the air and hear in it the bleakness of icy landscapes, the stillness of frozen lakes, and all the "northerness" that inspired it.

We complain of the material world, the risks it imposes and the suffering it brings; yet we love its flavors, sights, sounds, and sensations. It is not simply that bodies can touch, but that minds may meet, and meaning be discerned, and truth recognized, and beauty delighted in, and visions cherished. Even matters of necessity may be made lovely, and mechanical functions become an enchantment.

"THE NECESSARY EMBRACE OF BREEDING"

Think, for example, of the animal appetite by which we preserve and increase our kind. Beastly in origin, it may be humanly elevated to become a selfless devotion, an utterance of love, an awakening of adoration, an endless pleasure, and the impulse of the creative spirit. The "necessary embrace of breeding" becomes "beautiful also as fire," so that all music, art, poetry, and religion is quickened by what began as a hunger of our animal nature.

Or think of what we have done with "the survival of the fittest," a phrase commonly used to describe "nature red in tooth and claw" and the life of the unfit as "solitary, poor, nasty, brutish, and short." Yet not long ago I listened to a man who knows as much about Darwin as any man alive, and I heard him say that by reason of our care for those who are old, ill, or afflicted, the phrase "survival of the fittest" is no longer useful in much of our human society. It has been rendered obsolete by human compassion.

This means that in all our judgments we must take into account, not only what is natural to animals, but what belongs to our human nature; not only the laws of nature that describe behavior appropriate to beasts, but "natural law" that upholds the sort of conduct that befits rational and moral creatures with their innate demand for fairness, respect for truth, and regard for love.

CREDIT CARDS AND VALUES

Yet another instance of the way in which material stuff is elevated to spiritual significance is that it presses on us the necessity of moral choice. For a materialist is not merely someone who is aware that matter is the stuff of the world; he is someone who believes that this material stuff is all the reality there is. This means that he may become miserly ("with eyes like little dollars in the dark") and evaluate his life solely by the abundance of things that he possesses. Or he may give himself over to sensuality or the pursuit of power. Yet there are others who esteem material substance as a bearer of spiritual meaning and who employ it in the service of a transcendent reality.

The use we make of matter reveals our view of life and exposes our values. Our monthly credit-card statement, for example, will not only show our monthly indebtedness, it will tell us all we need to know about what we think is of true worth. Our checkbook will reveal, not just our balance, but our priorities and all the things we have set our heart on. Our use of material substance will reveal our generosity or expose our selfishness, our restraint or indulgence. Character is shaped, not only by our relations with other persons, but by our relation to material things. "Substance abuse" is a term that may have a wider reference than is commonly attributed to it.

Scripture makes a clear distinction between what it calls "the works of the flesh," or "worldliness," and what it describes as "the harvest of the Spirit"—between the temporal "things that are seen" and the eternal "things that are unseen." It posits a contest that sets our lower nature, what it sometimes calls "the flesh," against our higher nature, or "the spirit."

Some have understood this to mean that matter is evil in itself and is therefore to be despised by those who profess religious faith and are truly "spiritual." This view of things has led to some grotesque interpretations of the material world and to a denial of the pleasures it affords. Some have regarded their bodies with disgust and have scorned all physical delight. They have rejected the beauty of nature and have distrusted all joy. They have spurned, not only those pleasures that are cruel or selfish or sordid, but have rejected pleasure itself.

PURITANS AND PLEASURE

The Puritans (to put it in an Irish sort of way) have enjoyed a bad press recently and for several centuries past. They have been caricatured as haters of pleasure of every sort. The libel is not true of all Puritans, and those who repeat the slanders are often ill-informed. Many Puritans were lovers of great literature, good food, fine wines, dancing, and all the loveliness of this world. When we are tempted to gather all Puritans into an indiscriminate condemnation, we should slow down a little, and spare a thought for John Milton, and ask how he could be accommodated in such a group.

Yet some Puritans did forget that God "has given us all things richly to enjoy" and set themselves above the verdict declared in the book of Genesis, "God saw everything that He had made, and behold, it was very good." They did not heed the truth so well put by an old professor of mine who used to say that on the Day of Judgment we shall be called to account, not only for those sins we have committed, but for those good gifts of God we have not enjoyed:

> The Puritan through life's sweet garden goes,
> And plucks the thorn, and throws away the rose.
> He thinks to please by this peculiar whim,
> The God who made and fashioned it for him.

BODY AND FLESH

The Scriptures, of course, are misinterpreted when they are made to justify any such view as this. When Paul, for example, speaks of "the flesh," he is not speaking of the body. By "the flesh" he means our lower nature, that part of us that takes the best and makes it into the worst by trivializing, distorting, and prostituting it. If the body is love, then "the flesh" is lust; if the body is faithfulness, then "the flesh" is adultery; if the body is worship, then "the flesh" is idolatry; if the body is a healthy diet, then "the flesh" is gluttony; if the body is appreciation, then "the flesh" is envy; if the body is considerateness, then "the flesh" is ruthless ambition; if the body is self-control, then "the flesh" is selfish indulgence; if the body is forgiveness, then "the flesh" is vindictiveness and revenge.

Paul tells us, indeed, that our bodies are "limbs and organs of Christ," that the physical self is the shrine of the indwelling Spirit of God and is therefore to be held in honor. What else could Paul have said, for he knew that when God came into our world to show us how much He loved us, the Word was made flesh, and a human body bore the weight of glory.

Christians will not despise material substance, for they believe it to be God's creation. C. S. Lewis put it perfectly: "God likes matter. He invented it!"

"TO HIDE HIM ALL IT CAN"

There is yet another sublime use of the material world that begins for us in a story recounted in the book of Exodus. It tells how Moses, having asked to behold the glory of God, was not permitted to observe God coming, but was allowed to see Him going. He could not gaze upon the divine countenance, but caught a glimpse of the departing form. It was for his own protection that Moses was denied what he had asked for, because no one could look upon the face of God and live. As we shield our eyes from the sun, so Moses covered his face from the Eternal One.

What are we to make of the story? One of the things we may make of it is to realize that it describes one of the problems God had in creating us. It is a difficulty well understood by parents and teachers who would like their children or pupils to achieve a measure of freedom and individuality. They want their charges to learn from them without being overwhelmed by them. So wise parents hold back, and good teachers learn how to defend their students against their own influence.

Just think of the problem that must make for Omnipotence! How can God, who is the fountain of all Being and who fills everything at all times, find room for other minds and spirits and allow them to be? How is He to keep them from being overwhelmed? It is clear that God must hide Himself; must become in some way veiled, must put a barrier of one sort or another between His offspring and Himself. But of what sort could such a barrier be?

There is a rich Jewish understanding of creation that sees it as being as much God's withdrawal as His action. If God filled everything how could there be any room for us or anything? So He withdrew Himself to keep His creatures far enough away that they could, as it were, have a life of their own. Dr. Farrer allows a rabbi of ancient time to explain it to us:

What did God do? He drew back the skirts of His glory, to make a little space where He was not; and there He created the world. And so, where the world is, there He is not. And that is why we look in vain for His hand in the chances of nature. Nevertheless (Blessed be He!) He has visited us with His loving kindness.

"HIDE AND GO SEEK!"

That is why God's world must often appear to us as if there were no God. It is the divine way of "standing a handbreadth off to give His children room to grow." Once again, the poet gets it exactly right. Listen to Robert Browning's bishop as he attempts to explain things to the questioning skeptic in *Bishop Blougram's Apology:*

> Some think, Creation's meant to show him forth:
> I say it's meant to hide him all it can,
> And that's what all the blessed evil's for.
> Its use in Time is to environ us,
> . . . with shield enough
> Against that sight till we can bear its stress.

Now, that's not a bad thought for us to keep in mind when we are tempted to complain that God seems far away or appears to be avoiding us, or that the animal part of our nature too easily overwhelms the human part, or that the spiritual often seems no match for the material, or that the downward pull of things is so much stronger than the upward lift, or that the best things are so much harder to nurture than the worst things are to enjoy, or that we so often seem to take one step forward and two steps back on our pilgrimage, or that "the road winds uphill all the way."

All this makes us wonder why God makes it so hard to discover Him, let alone trust and love Him. And the answer is that

He wants us to find Him by following the gleam, not by being knocked down and overpowered by His presence.

The Chaos of the World

We have been singing a kind of "Hymn to Matter," yet for all the truth and beauty of it, our question remains: why is it a material world with its accompanying chaos? Granted that it puts some distance between the Creator and the created, does it need to be so confused and harsh to do so? Why is the world as chaotic as it is? The natural evils of earthquake, flood, and fire go on all the time in one part of the world or other, so that the life of many is no hymn to matter but a shout of anger at "acts of God." And accidents happen, and things go wrong, and people get sick, and everybody dies.

Why should it be like this? If an orderly and providential Mind really is behind everything, should we not expect to discover order and providential care in everything. If, as we are told, in the beginning "the earth was without form and void," then we might be forgiven for thinking that things really haven't improved much.

Once again, a lot will depend on the nature of our expectations. C. S. Lewis tells us that the world is like a building; half the people who live in it think it is a prison while the rest believe it to be a five-star hotel. Those who think it a prison cannot get over how good things are, while those who think it a hotel are constantly complaining about the room service.

What is our expectation? We have models for the kind of world we should like it to be. Should it not run like a well-oiled machine, or like a Rolex watch, or like a super-computer with a chip off the old Block? What we want is reliability, order, set form, flawless and functional design, and beauty added just for the fun of it; and we become upset when we don't get it.

I have a watch that is not behaving well. A day ago it

stopped in the middle of the night when I wasn't keeping my eye on it, and a day earlier it gained two minutes, and the day before that it lost three. Off to the repair shop with it for cleaning and adjustment so that I can know the time while spending my time! That is what we expect, not only of our watch, but of our world.

Yet that is not our world, and never could have been our world, and cannot ever be our world. We insist on taking the world we have and ignoring its nature, the very nature that has brought us to life, that is flesh of our flesh and bone of our bone, and trying to make it into something it is not. Do we not see that a world of turbines, clockwork, or computers could never have made us; nor could it have brought forth any of the qualities we most care about? Machines manufacture things, and watches mindlessly tick away, and computers tell us what we have told them to tell us. Our expectation is therefore disappointed. We should be pleased that it is, for the world we wish for is neither possible nor desirable.

"THE JUNGLE IS NEUTRAL"

Spencer Chapman was a British officer who lived and fought alone in the Malayan jungle during the Second World War. For several years he waged a successful solitary action against the occupying Japanese forces, disrupting their lines of communication and working as much mischief as he could to annoy and confuse them.

When he returned to England after the war, he was often asked whether the jungle was his friend or his foe; had he thought of it as being for him or against him? His answer became the title of the splendid book in which he recounted his adventures. He called it, *The Jungle Is Neutral*. The jungle, he wrote, was neither for him nor against him. It was itself. The ability to survive and fight depended on his skill in understanding the jungle's own nature and in using it to his own advantage. Its very neutrality meant that he could count on its always being itself, so that the better he understood it, the more useful it became.

Spencer Chapman's insight might be of some help to those of us who complain of nature's neutrality, her disinterestedness, her seeming indifference to moral questions and values, her failure to exhibit any particular care for the virtuous or distaste for the wicked. Like "Ol' Man River," she seems content to "Jes' keep rollin' along," unconcerned about good and evil and blind to justice and injustice alike.

THE KINDNESS OF INDIFFERENCE

We think it would be better if it were not so, if the earthquake had a conscience and the flood a moral sense, if the typhoon could make ethical distinctions and recognize both the kind and the cruel, if the laws of nature would bend a little to accommodate our purposes and vindicate our virtue. Would it not be a fine thing if the law of gravitation, for example, would behave in one way for a falling apple and in quite another for a falling airplane? It could then allow one to grow into a tree and save the other from tragedy.

Before we get quite carried away, we should notice that when Jesus spoke of the disinterestedness of nature it was not to lament her indifference but to praise her constancy. He seemed to think, indeed, that the evenhandedness of nature was a gift of grace, an expression of the divine goodness and generosity of "your Heavenly Father" who "makes His sun rise on good and bad alike, and sends His rain on the honest and the dishonest."

It is this constancy of nature, this being herself, that constitutes her character and allows us to understand her. Knowing her, we learn to count on and predict her behavior and use it to our own ends. If she were not constant enough to be understandable, if she did not answer to our thought of her, then the whole scientific enterprise would prove impossible. We may lament the law of gravitation that pulls the airplane out of the sky, yet it was only by understanding the same law that we were able to make it fly in the first place. If penicillin cured on one day and killed on another, what use would it be to anyone? This belief in a rational, constant, and dependable world, capable of being understood, is one of the great gifts of religion to science; it is part of the heritage, often unrecognized and unacknowledged, that our scientists have received from the Scholastics.

It is because of this constancy of nature that we can go beyond Spencer Chapman's description of the jungle as "neutral"; for the jungle, or nature, is not exactly neutral but is firmly on the side of thought, patience, and respect. Nature has secrets to share; but they will not be discovered by the idly curious, the foolish, or the arrogant. They will be revealed only to the humble in spirit, to those who are wise enough to acknowledge who she is, and are teachable.

"THE FACTITUDE OF THINGS"

We must reconcile ourselves to what George Macdonald called "The Factitude of Things," for the world is what it is, and not something else. When someone told Thomas Carlyle that Margaret Fuller, the New England Transcendentalist, had said, "I accept the universe," he replied, "By God, she'd better!" I love the story of the woman who complained to her physician that she did not like the night air, only to be told that during certain hours of the twenty-four, night air is the only air there is!

What do we have, then? We have, as we said, an exploding star and a kind of frenetic, chaotic energy that has been going on ever since. We see it wherever we look; everything is pushing against everything else and is attempting to take over everything everywhere.

We notice it when we scrutinize the lawn with a critical eye, for the "Clover, Dandelion, and Wild Thyme Company" is planning a corporate takeover. We see it when we lie on the grass and give our attention to any square inch of earth, for all the tiny things are about their business as though their business were the only business in the world. When we rise from the grass to walk in the woods, the squirrels are chasing the chipmunks and are out to gain the whole world for themselves. Why, even the cedars and maples are pressing each other and causing their branches to twist and bend as they reach for every beam of sunlight.

I know a geologist who thinks that the world will be taken over by what he calls "crack plants." You know "crack plants" even if you do not know you do, for you have seen them when they have pushed their way through the pin-sized holes in our asphalt driveways; every spring they crumble a little concrete to find their blooming room. When I scramble over the limestone rocks by the lake, where one could not find so much as a thimbleful of soil, it is to discover a flower of yellow or blue, or a tiny cedar that has found a place to put down a root and show an evergreen leaf. Of course the birds have helped by putting them there, but the birds did it as they went about their own compelling business of hunting for worms and building nests.

PROVIDENCE AND PERFECTION

Where shall we stop in our celebration of this natural fervor? Shall we cease with what we see or with what we know but cannot see? Are we to think of the rise and fall of dinosaurs, the coming and going of dodos, and a million instances of change and adaptation? The vitality is in everything, everywhere, all the time—in atoms too tiny for the eye and in galaxies too vast for the imagination. And it goes on, for the most part, with little awareness of itself. It simply happens. Well, perhaps not simply, but it happens!

Indeed, we don't need to look outside ourselves to discover it; for we find this vigorous spirit in our own person, in the friends who love us, and in those who dislike and resist us. The tension and energy of it are everywhere: in our ambition, and sexuality, and imagination; in our striving for excellence, and sense of self, and moral indignation. And we are aware of it, and cherish it, and should hardly recognize ourselves apart from it.

Our mistake is to imagine that God's providence, His timely and beneficent care for His creation, means, or ought to mean, that He accomplishes the world's perfection without harm or hurt to any part of it. But what could such a perfection mean, and how could it ever be achieved, given the nature of the world? For what we encounter in the world "is not a choir of angels, but a war of atoms," as Dr. Farrer so splendidly puts it; not a precise, inevitable, automated, programmed, machine-like process, but a magnificent, startling, diverse, and unwearied drama of birth and death, love and hate, glory and tragedy. Divine providence is not another name for perfection.

CHESS OR JAZZ?

Not long ago, Dr. Stephen Jay Gould of Harvard spoke of several recent discoveries in science that so astonished the scientific community as to set them chattering and making the headlines of the nation's newspapers. Professor Gould was not himself surprised at what had been discovered, and tells us why. It was because he had a different worldview, a dissimilar general model of reality. The older stories were well suited to a more stately, predictable, and comforting view than his own, which was decidedly unstately, quirky, and chancy. Gould saw a world of stunning and fascinating chaotic complexity, a universe of "multifarious intrigue." In his view, each of the lineages being discussed had its own idiosyncrasies, its own random effects, its own historical individuality and unpredictable future. I think Professor Gould might say of reality what Richard Holbrooke once said of diplomacy—that it is more like jazz than chess.

It may appear strange and inconsistent that we who in the next chapter of this book (see "The Mind of the World") will unequivocally reject chance as an explanation of anything and will affirm that neither we, nor anything else, can exist "by chance," should appear to be receptive to Professor Gould's view that reality is quirky and chancy, characterized by chaotic complexity and multifarious intrigue. Are we not seeking "to justify the ways of God to men" and defend the divine ordering of the world? If we are, then to be hospitable to Dr. Gould's views will seem an odd way of doing so. It may be appropriate enough for Dr. Gould to speak as he does of the nature of reality; but he is, by his own admission, an agnostic Jew, while we are Christian believers. Should we be sharing his vocabulary and catching his excitement?

Indeed we should, and that for three reasons: The first is that his worldview appears better able to account for the reality it seeks to accommodate and describe. Because of it, he was not surprised by the new discoveries that so astonished other scientists. The second is that it expresses what he calls "the messy and personal side of science" and places scientists among the creative artists who prize both truth and beauty. The third reason why Professor Gould's worldview is no threat to faith is that the providence in which we believe and wish to affirm is not merely a suggestion, a question, a hypothesis, or an article of faith. Providence is a fact. The proof of it is that anything exists. If there were no providential care, then nothing would be. God's heedfulness of His world is the infinite skill by which He allows His creation, from its smallest indeterminate impulses of energy to its heavens of stars, to go on being itself and making itself while He invisibly draws order from its chaos and beauty from its travail.

For how are we to doubt Providence when we have real existences? Is not our own being proof of the divine leading? Is not our world more predictable than not, and is not nature kind to us by a splendid disinterestedness? And if it is our lament that everyone dies, what is that but our acknowledgment that life is too good to lose? We are back to our protest that the food is bad and the portions small.

SAFETY LAST!

Given the sort of world we have, it is clear that the safety of its inhabitants cannot be its first concern. For one thing, there are natural evils to contend with. The enormous energies released in forming the earth, and the residue that continues in its physical nature, will account for many of the "acts of God" that can be so destructive of life and property. Volcanoes erupt here and earthquakes occur there; flood and fire afflict us along with the "thousand natural shocks that flesh is heir to." Why, we have even learned to arrange our hurricanes alphabetically and have names chosen for them before they arrive, as we have for our children.

As well as having natural evils we must contend with, ours is a world in which we hurt one another by the moral evil of which we all are capable and guilty. The useful energy of desire may get out of hand and render our ambition ruthless, and the appetite for power may become voracious. Our proper sense of self may deteriorate to an improper pride, and our concern for security to a crass indifference to the needs of others. We are sometimes cruel and selfish and cause each other much distress.

The question is whether we would wish our world to be other than it is; for if safety is not the world's priority, nor the priority of its Maker, neither is it our own highest value. We complain about the risks to life and limb in a world of this sort and then go off to climb mountains, cross oceans, traverse deserts, drop into caves, dive into lakes, leave vapor trails in the sky, soar into space, and ride to the moon. Courage, valor, loyalty, adventure, love—we honor these and a hundred other elements of character more highly than we value safety. Self-preservation is not our noblest concern.

A Jonik cartoon in a recent *New Yorker* shows us the highway signs that greet motorists and welcome them to "Insuranceville U.S.A." One declares a speed limit of ten miles per hour. Another announces: "No Fireworks; Seatbelts Required; No Tree Climbing; Bike Helmets Required; No Skating or Running; No Swimming; No Smoking; No Ball Playing; No Alcohol; No Fires; No Powertools; No Ladders; No Sharp Objects." It is all very amusing; yet cartoons manage to engage us, not only by their wit and humor, but by their proximity to truth.

Not long ago, a mother wrote an article for the *Wall Street Journal* in which she lamented that we have made life so safe for our children that many of the adventures that were the delight of her own childhood, and are now the stuff of some of her happiest memories, are no longer possible for her own brood, for the law will no longer permit them.

She mentioned the absence of wooden swings and seesaws from our parks, and car seats that force infants to stare backward at upholstery for the duration of any trip they take. Kids are no longer permitted to go poking around construction sites and are forbidden to play in alleys. Yet the "shining of remembered days" that includes these hazardous pursuits is dear to many of us, and the most memorable occasions were those that had an edge of uncertainty and danger to them.

Besides this, a million benefits have come to us from the menacing nature of the world, not the least of them being the whole scientific enterprise to understand and control it. Enormous energies are required at all levels of existence to sustain the created order; and if we sometimes think the vitality too much, or a little rough, we must surely think a little much better than not enough. Who among us would wish for a tame and domesticated world? If that were our wish, and if we were so unfortunate as to have it granted, vigor would be lost from the natural world and zest from our own nature.

DWARFED OR SMOTHERED?

I have never been able to understand, for example, the complaint of those who say that the universe is so vast that they are made to feel totally overwhelmed and insignificant by it. I remember Chesterton's comment that if it is size that overwhelms us, a whale will do almost as well as a universe. Do we imagine that we'd be more at home if the universe were a little smaller, cozier, and more manageable? But why should we think so?

When I was a boy, I often walked to what we called "The Valley." It was a wood near my home with a stream running through it and steep banks that in springtime were covered with primroses and bluebells. For a young boy it was a place of enchantment. But one day I not only walked into The Valley, I walked out of it on the far side and discovered not only where it began but where it ended. I learned its dimensions and discovered that it did not go on forever.

In that moment, some of the allure and mystery went out of it. Part of its enchantment was that I had thought it endless. It wasn't. It was neither infinite nor eternal. Blaise Pascal was among those who complained that the size of the universe terrified him. It doesn't have that effect on me because I remember The Valley and know how much better it is to be dwarfed than smothered. I would rather be overwhelmed by vastness than suffer from cosmic claustrophobia.

THE BEST OF ALL IMPOSSIBLE WORLDS?

But we have a further question about the kind of world we wish our world to be. We should ask, not only if it is desirable, or ought to be desired, but whether it is even possible that it could exist. The easy answer is, of course, a flight to Omnipotence. If God is omnipotent then surely any kind of world is possible. But we have already seen that omnipotence does not mean that. Such a world as we should like to have is possible only if God wishes it to be, because power, even absolute power, cannot accomplish what it has no wish to accomplish. But besides this, there is another reason such a world as we posit does not exist: it may not be a possible world; it may hold fatal contradictions in itself and contain incompatible requirements.

When I was a child, it afforded my chums and me much pleasure to ask questions we knew to be foolish. Yet silly as they were, they taught us the good lesson that some questions are meaningless. The only answer they can receive is an answer as silly as the question itself. The questions began simply, but became more difficult and finally acquired a theological tone.

"The Length of a Piece of String"

One question, "How high is up?" received the answer, "The length of a piece of string." Another wanted to know, "What shape is pink?" and another "How many minutes are there in a mile?" Or we might ask, "Could God make a stone so heavy that not even He could lift it?" Yet another inquired about the divine skill in making triangles with four sides, round squares, or square circles. It was foolish and fun. We even made it into a jingle of silliness:

> A fire in the ocean; A blind man saw it;
> A man with no legs ran to get the fire-brigade;
> The fire-brigade came round the corner as fast as a funeral;
> It ran over two dead cats and killed them.

The trouble is that some of us have carried the game into adult life and have forgotten both the lesson it taught and that it is a game. So we ask our nonsense questions and challenge God to answer them; and when He does not, we conclude that He lacks the skill to do so. They are too hard for Him. What we ought to remember is that if such questions are not answered it is because they are unanswerable, for they are nothing but bits of verbal nonsense.

What we should like is a world orderly enough to be predictable, yet spontaneous enough to adapt itself to our eccentric desires and erratic behavior. We want a law of gravitation that is constant enough for us to learn the rules of flight, yet we wish it to abandon its own nature when bodies fall out of the sky. We want a world of turbulent, impersonal, disinterested natural forces that will not hurt anybody, a material world of soft bodies and hard rocks in which no one will ever take any hard knocks and accidents will never occur. We wish for a world in which love is possible and hurt is not, in which lips are sensitive enough for kisses but are insensible to pain.

In a recent movie, Sean Connery, who plays King Arthur, asks Richard Gere, who plays Sir Lancelot, if he has ever been afraid. When Lancelot answers that he has not, the king replies, "Then you have never loved."

The king is right, as kings ought to be. Is it possible to love and not know fear? Can we, do you think, discover sympathy in a world without suffering or compassion in a world without pain? Can we have learning without discipline or fortitude without hardship? Do we really desire the bliss of ignorance or the cheerful unawareness that signals our lack of imagination? Do we still think it better to have loved and lost than never to have loved at all?

What is worth noticing is that while we object to the hardness of the world, we like to talk about it once our bit of hardship is over. An old proverb puts it perfectly, "What was hard to endure is sweet to recall." We are like the salty old sea captain who admitted that while he didn't like being in a storm at sea, he liked having been in a storm at sea. The reason for this is that the person who has come through a storm is usually not the same person who went into it. Demanding experiences may leave us better men and women because of the demands they make of us.

EASY COURAGE?

It is not hard to understand why the distressing experiences we pass through can yield enduring benefits: it is because most of the qualities we covet can be gained only in difficult circumstances. There is no such thing as easy courage, for example; courage is always difficult. If it is easy, it is hardly courage; for in order to be courageous, we must first be afraid. Being courageous does not mean that we are not afraid; it means that we are afraid but refuse to allow our fears to determine our actions. And that is so hard that only courage can do it!

This is one of the reasons we must be careful not to wish for desirable qualities without some reckoning of their cost. It was Hemingway who defined fortitude as "grace under pressure," which means, for one thing, that if we want the fortitude we should get ready for the pressure. How are we to learn the meaning of hope without being close to despair, or discover the value of freedom if there is never a threat to our liberty? If we wish to be heroic we must spurn self-pity, and if we hanker after self-reliance we had better not need frequent reassurance. We can't be forgiving without having something to forgive, and that could mean a wounded spirit or a broken heart.

I read of a man who grew impatient with his own impatience and asked God to help him get rid of it. Next morning, he missed his train. He had hoped for a less immediate and less trying answer than that, but what other kind of answer is possible?

We learn to be patient only in circumstances that try our patience and invite our impatience. We must be careful what we ask for, because getting it may cost us more than we expect or are willing to pay.

Everything will depend on whether we believe character to be more important than comfort. If God thinks it is, then it goes a long way towards justifying the sort of world He has made for us. If He denies us peace, perhaps it is because He would give us glory!

WHAT MOTHER TERESA DID NOT UNDERSTAND

If our discussion of the physical nature of the world seems more theoretical than practical, we should bring the point of it home by applying it to an unhappy event that wrenched the hearts of everybody in the world. When Mother Teresa was told of the death of Princess Diana of Wales in a car crash in Paris, she responded by saying, "I do not understand the ways of God."

What did Mother Teresa mean? She may have been simply expressing her sense of shock and sorrow at the appalling news of the death of a young mother and princess. Or she might have been holding God and Diana together in her thoughts, so that her response was an act of trust in the divine goodness.

She might also have meant that she did not understand how the accident could have happened. But if that is what she meant, then we might wonder what there was about the accident that was so hard to understand. If passengers without seat belts are driven at an excessive speed by a driver who has been drinking and is attempting to outrun newsmen and photographers who respect no limits in pursuing their quarry, it should not be difficult to understand how the accident could occur. How could it not?

Of course, Mother Teresa's comment might mean something

deeper than that, for it might really be a question asking why this is the sort of world in which accidents happen, or why it is a physical world in which hard metal crushes fragile bodies? If this is what Mother Teresa was asking, then these are the very questions we have been attempting to answer, and the practical application of our arguments will be apparent.

CHAPTER NINE

THE MIND
OF THE WORLD

ON NOT CHANCING IT

T here is another account of the origin of the world that says it got its start, neither in what a single mind intended nor in the crossed purposes of two minds in conflict, but in the purposelessness of no mind at all. For the world is mindless. It was created by chance. Now, if this were true, then the problem of evil would no longer exist; for which of us would feel any need to make sense of a world we knew to be senseless?

This view of things resurfaced not long ago when an English astrophysicist wrote an article in which he scolded those scientists, poets, and philosophers who speak of purpose in the universe. He told them to save their breath to cool their porridge, for that kind of talk is silly. He rebuked Stephen Hawking for daring to think of "knowing the mind of God" as he sought to discover the meaning of the cosmos. This scientist said that the universe has no meaning and no purpose. Life, and human intelligence, exist only by chance. We are here by chance.

Now what is this "chance" by which we are brought to life and being? The English scientist speaks of it as though it were a grand design, an all-embracing purpose that conceives and directs and is the reason for everything. Some chance! We had always thought that chance is the absence of intentional action. It isn't an explanation, it is the absence of explanation. Now, suddenly, we are to believe that chance creates and explains everything. I believe such a way of talking is nonsense, and I think I can prove it to you.

Suppose I were to describe a social event, say a wedding that I attended, by writing an account of it for the local paper. I might say that the catering was by McDonald's, the groom's suit by Eddie Bauer, and the bride's gown by L. L. Bean. So far, so good! But suppose I went on to say that the bride's hair was styled "by chance." What would you make of that? I think you would not be able to make anything of it. You would conclude that I was trying to be funny and that the bride's hair was in a state of disarray and had not been styled at all. Chance cannot style anything, yet here we are being confidently invited by a man of science to attribute the beginning of everything to something that couldn't arrange a young woman's hair! Goethe once exclaimed, "Woe to him who would ascribe something like reason to Chance and make a religion of surrendering to it!"

I know a historian who says that chance is a mask and that it is the historian's task to tear it away. He attempts to lift it off because it explains nothing, accounts for nothing. To say that something happened by chance is to say that it happened. The words "by chance" add nothing to our understanding of how or why it happened. They not only fail as explanation but are useless as description. Chance explains nothing, but is itself in need of explanation. We hope to be rid of it once we have discovered what it is hiding.

THE PURPOSE OF PURPOSES

That sly old fox, Robert Frost, once asked a group of students who had gathered in a famous New England college to hear him read his poetry, "Does the universe have a purpose?" They thought about that and decided it didn't. He then asked them, "Are you capable of having purposes?" They thought they were.

The poet then wanted to know if they thought that the purpose of the universe might be that they should have purposes? Now, that's a good question. Our English astrophysicist wrote, "In a very real sense, the universe doesn't have any meaning." Now isn't that an odd sentence! If the universe doesn't have a meaning, how can we speak of anything having "a very real sense"? Any "real sense" is surely a hint of meaning. If we find "real sense" anywhere, should we not regard it as an invitation to look for it everywhere?

It is not that purposes in a purposeless universe have no point to them; they have too much point to them! It is not that minds in a mindless world do not make sense, they make too much sense! It is hard to believe that minds were created mindlessly or that our ability to act purposefully was brought about accidentally. To believe that is like saying that while Lady Macbeth is capable of acting with cunning deliberation and manipulative skill, the play *Macbeth* is the work of a chimpanzee.

How can we everywhere discover minds that are made, including our own, and deny the Mind of the Maker? How can we experience a rational world and consider its origin irrational; or believe that the universe, which seems more and more like a great thought, is the result of "two blind children, chance and accident, making mud pies in the dark"? Frost couldn't make that add up and wrote an amusing poem about it, and called it, "Accidentally On Purpose." It ends by saying:

> Grant me intention, purpose and design—
> That's near enough for me to the Divine.

NOTHING LESS THAN PERSONAL!

People sometimes tell me they believe in "Something" (with a capital *S*), but that they don't believe in a personal God. They thus deny to God the attributes, qualities, and values that make us personal: thought, will, intention, self-awareness, love, creativity, humor, freedom. Such talk is silly, for if God does not possess these attributes, He is less personal than we are, which means that He is no God at all. That kind of explanation explains nothing. It is to attribute personality to Mickey Mouse and deny it to Walt Disney; it is to say that Hamlet is more personal than Shakespeare, and that the Muppets possess more creativity than Jim Henson. It is to credit Scrooge and Tiny Tim with more individuality than Charles Dickens.

A CLUB FOR DINOSAURS

Not long ago, while watching the Discovery Channel, I discovered that there was a time in the history of dinosaurs when they began to change rapidly. They grew bigger, for one thing, and their basic nature was exaggerated. The aggressive ones became more aggressive and the defensive ones more defensive. The vegetarians ate more vegetables, and the carnivores ate more vegetarians. One of the defensive ones went so far as to grow a club at the end of its tail with which it proceeded to bash anything that looked at it with bad intent.

Now, who thought of a tail like that? Did the dinosaur? And if it did, was the thought of it powerful enough to ensure its growth? Does dinosaur wishing really make it so? The explanation mentioned in passing was that the tail "evolved," which means, I suppose, that some genetic mechanism passed the word that a club was needed, and what was needed was provided.

The "explanation" may be true. Indeed, I am inclined to think it true. Except that it is not an explanation. It just changes the question and adds to its complexity. Now I hardly care where the club came from; what really interests me is where the hereditary mechanism that produced it came from! How did it know to establish and preserve those functions most necessary to survival? Did someone tell it how to do so? Or if, as we are sometimes told, everything was accomplished by "natural selection," how and where did the selection find its nature?

We may say that things simply evolved like that; but "simply evolved" is not as simple as it sounds. Why did they evolve like that? No doubt, everything has a mechanism of some sort by which it works, for everything must work in some way. Nothing works in no way. But how are we to account for the mechanism? How does it know to work in the way it works? Is there, as the poet believes, a Presence, a Mind, "too instant to be known," perfectly hidden in creation?

> The silent mover of the play,
> The focus of its myriad parts—

One day during the summer I went walking by the lake. The sun was warm, but not too hot; and the breeze was cool, but not too cold; and I thought to myself what a miracle it was to be so nicely placed in so perfect a temperature. The small wonder suggested a larger one: that the earth seems to be exactly the right distance from the sun. A little closer and we'd perish by fire; a little farther away, by ice.

I also found myself wondering how a reductionist of the sort we have considered might reply if I dared tell him my thoughts. I should imagine he would explain that my sense of wonder was misplaced and inappropriate. Had it not occurred to me that if the distance between earth and sun hadn't been right to begin with there could have been no life at all and we shouldn't be around to wonder at the sun on our face?

But that is no explanation at all. The truth is that he has said exactly the same thing to me that I said to him. Except that he calls it an explanation; and speaks with the condescension of one who knows; and thinks these poets, philosophers, and musicians an odd lot.

CHARACTERS OUT OF CONTROL

John Moffit's phrase, "the silent mover of the play," gives us another reason to place Mind or Spirit at the center of our thought of creation. It suggests that God makes the world as a novelist makes characters or as a dramatist crafts *dramatis personae*. Such creation is neither remote for the Creator nor passive for the created. It is, like some of our telephone calls, person-to-person.

Richard Strauss and Hugo von Hofmannsthal discovered this when their opera *Der Rosenkavalier* resisted all their efforts to make it what they had intended it to be. The composer and librettist had thought to write a thoroughly comic opera, "as bright and obvious as a pantomime," but it did not turn out that way. When they got into their work, the Marschallin, who in their original intent had no claim to either distinction or preeminence, captured their imagination and took them over. She inspired their best lines and their most sublime music in such a way as to reshape her own character and transform the nature of the work. The opera was now closer to tragedy than to comedy; it was more dark than bright, more profound than lightsome.

If that is how the Maker of heaven and earth creates, then He must be at it all the time. His supreme skill is not in merely making things, but in allowing things to make themselves. Martin Buber states it splendidly:

> It is senseless to ask how far my action reaches, and where God's grace begins. . . . What concerns me alone before I bring something about, is my action, and what concerns me alone, when the action is successfully done, is God's grace.

He goes on to say that one action is not less real than the other, and neither is part-cause; for while man's action is enclosed in God's action, it is still real action.

This means that He enables us to be truly ourselves, express-ing our own will, displaying our own character, acting from the inner consistency and necessity of our own nature. Yet at all times and in every moment He so encloses our action within His own as to not only form our character but give our charac-ter a formative part in His drama. The Prince of Denmark is both his own man and Shakespeare's Hamlet. The Marschallin belongs both to herself and to Richard Strauss. Paul puts it per-fectly for all who know the Creator Spirit: "I, yet not I, but the grace of God."

CHAPTER TEN

ANIMAL PAIN

*T*here are many who think the pain of animals a tougher problem for a merciful Providence and harder to reconcile with the kindness of God than the suffering of *Homo sapiens.* Their reasons are plain and have been plainly stated.

For one thing, "poor dumb animals" feel pain without being able to tell us that they do, or show us where it hurts, or describe how it feels. They cannot make sense of their pains or discover any meaning in them, and are therefore unable to draw any mitigating moral good out of them. Add to this that animals must be, with our own small children, the quintessential innocent sufferers; for they are not wicked or cruel or vicious, but for the most part innocently get on with defending and supporting their own lives, and preserving their own kind, in an animal sort of way. And then, of course, the sheer amount of animal pain seems overwhelming.

THE KINDNESS OF PAIN

These reasons appear compelling, yet we should resist the conclusion that animal pain, appalling as it is in both severity and amount, presents the greatest obstacle to belief in a kind and merciful Providence. For one thing, we must surely believe that for animals, as for humans, it is better to be than not to be. We may not wish to go as far as Wordsworth when he tells us it is his faith "that every flower enjoys the air it breathes."

Yet it is the animals themselves who seem to tell us that life is a great good, for they do all they can to preserve their own existence and to ensure the continuance of their kind. For the most part, their life is long and agreeable, and their dying short. We should notice, too, that pain is of great usefulness to them, as it is to us, even though they may not be aware that it is. It sounds an alarm, for example, telling us that something is wrong; and it compels us to protect our injured part, thus giving it a chance to heal and recover. Or it slows us down and forces us to bed when we might otherwise use up, in less important ways, the valuable energy needed to combat the sickness that has attacked us. If there were no pains from injuries, then both humans and animals might do great damage to themselves without knowing they were doing it.

Not long ago, after a brief engagement with my dentist, I managed to chew up my lip. He had frozen it so that he could painlessly get on with his work, and I foolishly attempted coffee and a donut while it was still numb. Silly me! I could bite my lip without the slightest discomfort. But the painlessness was no longer a benefit, but a hazard, as I was to discover an hour later when my mouth thawed and sensation returned.

We dread the diseases that don't bother to tell us they are there until it is too late to do much about them. Then we feel that our body has betrayed us doubly: first by becoming ill, but also by not being courteous enough to mention it to us. Some illnesses are deadly because they are painless. The frightening thing about glaucoma, for example, is that it has no symptoms. We are not aware that we are suffering from it until blindness is upon us.

On Not Knowing When to Stop

The trouble with pain, of course, is that it doesn't know when to stop. It usefully sounds an alarm, but alarms that don't stop alarming drive us mad. As I write this, a car outside my window is going through a round of startling sounds with a zeal and versatility to rival the brass section of the New York Philharmonic. I wish it would stop.

Pain is like that. It is kind enough to tell us that something is wrong, but is inconsiderate enough to keep on telling us what we already know. If only it would learn to blow its horn, wave its flag, ring its bell, flash its light, shout its warning, and then have the decency to quit!

It doesn't, of course; and we must think of what it would take for it to do so. The leg that hurts would have to possess, not only the capability to feel pain, but enough awareness of itself and of me to recognize that its message had been sent, received, and could be safely turned off. But to know this, it would need a brain of its own. Yet I have no wish for my limbs and organs to have minds of their own. Some of them might turn temperamental. I can imagine the stress fracture in my foot, or the crack in my elbow, saying to me, "I've told you there's something wrong. It hurts me to keep bringing it up. How often do I have to tell you, anyway?" The one thing I have no wish for is a foot or an elbow with an attitude. One center of self-awareness is enough.

NO SUM OF SUFFERING

There is another observation that may be of enormous comfort and reassurance as we deal with the ills that afflict us. It is that while in imagination we may attempt to add up all the pains of the animal and human populations of the world, in all places and at all times, such a sum of suffering does not and cannot exist. Pain is not accumulable, and our imagination does not serve us well when it tells us that it is.

How *can* there be a sum of suffering? Is there any way in which my toothache can be added to uncle Harry's earache and sister Margaret's arthritis to come up with a total amount of pain for all three? We may try to imagine such an amount, but can do so only vaguely, while the fact remains that no one bears either that or any sum of suffering. Each sufferer bears his own and will have sympathy both for the others and from the others, but no one will bear the suffering of all three.

George Bernard Shaw once wrote that "what one person can suffer is the maximum that can be suffered on earth." The Argentinean poet and philosopher Jorge Louis Brogues happily quotes Shaw and goes on to say that "there is no point in being overwhelmed by the appalling total of human suffering" since such a total does not exist. "Neither poverty nor pain is accumulable," he tells us.

C. S. Lewis, in *The Problem of Pain,* similarly urges us not to make the problem of pain worse than it is by vague talk about "the unimaginable sum of human misery," for that composite pain cannot be found in anyone's consciousness. There is no such thing as "a sum of suffering" for the simple reason that no one suffers it: "When we have reached the maximum that a single person suffers . . . we have reached all the suffering there can ever be in the universe."

Yet there is One who suffers the sum of the anguish of this world: It is God Himself; for He knows each of His children and all of His creatures with an immediacy more instant and acute than their own consciousness of themselves, and feels their suffering more deeply than they do in their own person. George Macdonald puts it bluntly:

> Of all teachings that which presents a far distant God is the nearest to absurdity. Either there is none, or He is nearer to any one of us than our nearest consciousness of self.

This enables us to better understand what it means to say of God, "surely He hath borne our griefs and carried our sorrows."

If there is a sum of suffering, it is not made by a human mind, nor is it known in any human experience, but in the mind and heart of God. Only He can know the pain of this world, and only He can bear it. Yet it is we who complain of it! We hold it against Him as a reason for unbelief while all the time it is He who carries it in love and redeems it by an infinite compassion. Why, not even a sparrow falls to the ground without our Heavenly Father knowing it:

> And can He who smiles on all
> Hear the wren with sorrows small,
> Hear the small bird's grief and care,
> Hear the woes that infants bear —
>
> And not sit beside the nest,
> Pouring pity in their breast,
> And not sit the cradle near,
> Weeping tear on infant's tear?

NOT ALL PAIN IS SUFFERING

When we speak of animal pain and attempt to relate it to both human suffering and divine providence, we are obliged to make a distinction between pain and suffering. We commonly use the words interchangeably to mean roughly the same thing; yet they do not mean the same thing, and the difference in their meaning is important in this present context.

Not all pain is suffering, and not all suffering is caused by bodily pain. Pain is a physical sensation of discomfort, which may be felt in varying degrees of severity and duration. Suffering, on the other hand, is not a physical sensation at all but a condition of mental or moral or spiritual distress. It would be impossible to mention every ingredient of its makeup, for it is as wide and deep, as subtle and varied as human experience itself. We suffer when we are afraid, bereaved, disappointed, uncertain, lonely, threatened, ashamed, humiliated, anxious, impoverished, or envious. Why, the components of it are limitless both in number and variety. Physical pain is often an important part of suffering and may indeed be the chief cause of it. Yet all pain is not suffering. I proved this to myself not long ago when I attempted to dash across a New York street, but instead tripped and fell, and went into the curb like a baseball player stealing second base. I picked myself up, dusted myself off, and went on with what it was I had to do. An hour or so later my arm began to hurt, and a trip to the emergency room of my local friendly hospital revealed that it was broken.

Now, I had to put up with a little hurt; but to describe it as suffering would be to so exaggerate it as to distort it. What I had to deal with was a bit of physical pain, easily bearable, that was not the occasion of suffering.

Of course I was annoyed at myself for not acting my age by sprinting across uneven streets; and the inconvenience of spending time and energy on the injury made me impatient; and I hated suffering a loss of dignity and a measure of embarrassment. But even to mention these things is to make too much fuss about them. What happened to me was a pain, and little more than that.

SUFFERING IS NOT ALL PAIN

When we speak of suffering, it is to imagine physical pain so great as to tempt one to despair; or grief so deep as to rob the days of their music; or anxiety so severe as to turn life into a miserable foreboding; or fear so pervasive as to cripple our initiative and steal our hope. Those who suffer mental illness often endure no physical pain at all, yet their suffering may be so severe that their days become an unending and inescapable nightmare.

The suffering that would be truly tormenting would be to realize that we had embarrassed others by our foolishness, or betrayed them by our cowardice, or dismissed them by our indifference, or destroyed them by our callousness, or crushed them by our insensitivity, or sacrificed them to our appetites, or exploited them by our ruthlessness, or manipulated them by our power. No physical pain need be any part of these appalling attitudes and dispositions, yet the suffering would be enormous.

When we talk like this, what strikes us most about animal pain is its simplicity. It does not carry the enormous moral and emotional load we have recognized as being part of human suffering. Mark Twain was right when he reminded us that humans are the only animals that blush, or need to. Pascal is sure that only man can be "great in his misery," and Santayana wonders whether the only true dignity of man is in his capacity to despise himself. These are regions of the human spirit that are not part of animal nature.

There is no guilt or shame in animal pain. As Walt Whitman tells us, the animals do not lie awake in the dark and weep for their sins. Nor should they, for they are animals and guilt is no part of their makeup. Nor does their death cast a long shadow over their life, for they hardly think of it until it is upon them.

To say this does not mean that we are unsympathetic; it is simply to acknowledge that animals suffer as animals, not as persons. We may say of our pets that they are almost human, or that they come close to the achieving of personality; yet they are not human, and so they have their own pains but not our suffering.

Our poets have not only known this, but have expressed it with gentleness, power, and beauty. When Robert Burns turned over the nest of a mouse with his plough in the autumn of 1785, he responded by writing one of his tenderest poems, lamenting the ruin of the tiny hard-won hearth and home and affirming his kinship with the small creature. They are fellow mortals, are they not? Yet in the end, he thinks the mouse better off than he is, because touched only by present time. Not so the poet:

> Still thou art blest, compared wi' me!
> The present only toucheth thee:
> But, och! I backward cast my e'e
>   On prospects drear!
> An' forward though I canna see,
>   I guess an' fear!

Yeats has the same thought. Only humans know what it is to die. The anticipation of death belongs only to humankind. A dying animal perishes without dread or hope. Not so the human animal, who anticipates death and awaits it with foreboding and hope:

> He knows death to the bone—
> Man has created death.

CHAPTER ELEVEN

"CONFESSION IS GOOD FOR THE SOUL"

NOTHING IS AS IT SHOULD BE

e have talked about evil as we encounter it in the natural world: in animal pain and in flood, earthquake, and fire; and we have spoken of our "too, too solid flesh" afflicted by disease, weakened by age, and finally, dissolved by death. We must now consider a form of evil that is more pervasive and universal even than ill health or natural disaster, and is known and felt with a more instant personal immediacy and a greater sense of individual responsibility. I mean, of course, the moral evil we know at first hand because we are guilty of it. It is not simply that bad things happen, but that we ourselves make them happen and are to blame for them.

When we say of our world that "nothing is as it should be," we are describing, not merely a universe outside our own person, but a world of which we ourselves are a part, in whose wickedness we are implicated, and for which we must accept some measure of responsibility. Years ago a British newspaper offered a prize for the best short letter telling what was wrong with the world. Chesterton won it by writing a terse and playful note that said:

Dear Mr. Editor,

I am.

Yours faithfully,

G. K. Chesterton

The varieties of human wickedness are numberless, and the nuances of culpability both mysterious and infinite. We may cheat, steal, lie, hate, or murder. We may behave so badly, so consistently, and for so long, that we may worsen into bad characters whose defining characteristic is their wickedness. We may be known as cruel, cowardly, dishonest, or simply evil. When Sir Winston Churchill attempted to describe the vileness of Adolf Hitler and could find no word to match the evil of which he was guilty, he called him "that bad man."

THE MEANING OF CHARACTER

As soon as we mention character we have a sense of something uniquely valuable that has to be striven for, can be preserved only with vigilance, and is in constant danger of being lost. We speak of it as "our" character, but character is not anything we have, but something we are. Our character, like our soul, is simply our own self.

We commonly use a cluster of words to describe the moral tension out of which character is formed, by which it is sustained, and through which it may be forfeited. They speak of a moral sense and expectation—of temptation, betrayal, guilt, judgment, consequences, punishment. Words like these remind us that our life is a drama, not a process; that it is best interpreted, not by the categories of the sciences, hard or soft, but in a vocabulary that is personal, individual, and dramatic.

"THE PLAY'S THE THING"

If our life is a drama rather than a process, then it will not surprise us that all the serious playwrights in the world's history have attempted to set that drama before our eyes. They all have known that because character matters supremely, the real battles are always about keeping or losing one's true self. That is why the stage drama does not belong to the tragic hero alone; it is our drama too, for the hero's soul is not more valuable than our own.

And that is why we leave the theater elevated, however dark the tragedy; for we have been reminded of our stature as moral beings and of the enormous significance of the moral choices we make day in and day out. The opposite to the tragic view of life is not the comic view, but the trivial view. Whatever other props and bits of scenery furnish the set, the true setting of all drama is a moral expectation, an ethical demand, a requirement of conscience that the self must either fulfill or be lost. Lacking this, the play holds little interest. As Chesterton put it, "Books without morality in them are books that will send you to sleep standing up."

THE NATURE OF OUR COMPLAINT

Our complaint about God's way with His world will not be lacking in interest then, for it is concerned with morality in at least two senses: not only is it a complaint about the nature, variety, and amount of moral evil, but is itself an instance of our complicity in it and an example of our entanglement with it.

We express our dissatisfaction with God's manner of managing the world by becoming angry with Him. We rail against Him and assail His honor over every natural disaster, every personal injustice, every social tragedy that comes within range of our attention. With all the modern means of spreading bad news, that is a very wide range indeed. We ascend the moral high ground and stand like Moses on Sinai, only not delivering ethical insights, but demanding a clear, complete, and satisfactory moral explanation of the world's ills. We may even threaten to stop believing in Him if He doesn't come through. We make Thomas Carlyle's grievance our own, and complain that God sits in heaven and does nothing.

Yet our sound and fury may signify nothing, for our moral outbursts are sometimes a conceit and a deception. It is within our power to relieve many of the troubles we complain about, yet we choose not to. It is not God who does nothing, but we ourselves. God has placed in our own hands the means to assuage many of the evils we deplore. Yet for all the fierceness of our moral indignation, we are often unwilling to devote our time, or thought, or energy, or money to relieving the afflictions of others. It is easier to blame God for the distress of the world than to become an instrument of His goodness.

THE FREEDOM TO CHOOSE

Yet even the exposure of our insincerity may lead to a further charge against the Almighty, for we may require Him to tell us why He allows our minds to be so obtuse, our hearts so unfeeling, our wills so nerveless. If our hearts are hard, then it must be because God has hardened them as, we are told, He hardened Pharaoh's heart against the just claims of Israel in Egypt.

Why does God allow us to be so mean, selfish, uncaring, and self-serving? We are not all of these things all of the time, but we are some of these things some of the time. If only God had made us better, then we would be better and the world would be a happier place. Why did He not? Why does He allow people to be the way they are? He should not have endowed us with so much independence when His omniscience must have let Him know that we weren't capable of handling it.

THE COURAGE TO BE

Of all our complaints against God, this must surely be the most ungrateful, the most unbecoming, and the most wayward, because it faults God for conferring upon us the single quality we most covet for our offspring. In raising the children of our heart, we attempt to nurture in them a deepening sense of their own worth and an increasing awareness of their own independence, freedom, and responsibility. We consider it our best and highest accomplishment that they should have minds of their own, be in possession of their own person, and learn to make discerning choices and responsible decisions for themselves. Their freedom is at once our finest gift and their own highest achievement, for it is the attribute that defines them as persons and makes possible every other quality and value they possess. Indeed, we should never have been able to accomplish it in them if God had not first achieved it in us. Yet, rather than thanking Him for having done so, we accuse Him of having done so. We hold it as a grievance against Him that He gives us the freedom to be ourselves.

What an odd lot we are! It is as though Gepetto the puppet-maker had expressed his delight that Pinocchio his puppet had become a person, but had then gone on to complain that he himself was a person and not a puppet!

WHAT WOULD WE HAVE HIM DO?

We wonder how anyone could think of acting so perversely; yet we are guilty of the same contrariness when we blame God for allowing us to misuse our freedom, forgetting that if He didn't allow us to misuse it, it wouldn't be freedom. What would we have Him do? Would we like Him to diminish it, or take it from us altogether?

Sometimes the only possible answer to our grievances would be for God to take us over and make us more like puppets than persons. But to do so would be to undo us, and thus deny the whole purpose of creation. If what God desires is that we should come to know and love Him, and if the highest achievement of personality is that we should freely choose to do so, then the expectation that it would help anything to strip us of our freedom is nonsensical.

Take, for example, the sad happening of which we have already spoken, the accident that proved fatal to Princess Diana and was so bewildering to Mother Teresa. We wonder why God did not do something to prevent it.

If our wondering means that we strongly wish the accident had never occurred, then it expresses a universal sentiment. But if it means literally what it says clearly, that God should have done something to stop it, and that His seeming paralysis is in fact culpable neglect, then we really must ask what we think He should have done.

At what time during the evening should God have come in and begun to assert Himself? In time to ensure that the driver did not have too much to drink? Or, failing that, should He have behaved like a good friend and confiscated the keys to the car? Should He have personally ensured that all seat belts were safely fastened? Should He have contrived to govern the speed of the Mercedes, or to immobilize the newsmen and photographers who pursued it? Ought He to have rendered concrete soft and steel pliable to prevent all injuries, or should He have healed them as they happened? Or why did He not simply raise the dead and give them back to each other and restore them to their friends that very evening? What we have suggested is not only a piece of nonsense, it is a grotesque piece of nonsense.

CONDEMNED TO BE FREE?

There are those who, having considered the state of the world and the harm we do to each other, talk about freedom as a burden. They might just as well speak of the self, or self-awareness, or life, as a burden. To wish to be rid of our freedom is, as we have seen, a wish to substitute a marionette, a dummy, a mannequin, for thought, character, humor, and all the richness of personal being. It might make for a safer world, but who would know, and who would care?

God would not improve us if He were to deprive us of our freedom; He would unmake us. If such a thing were to happen, the self would not be enhanced, but annihilated. We are not condemned to be free, for it is our freedom that defines what it means to be a person. In our silly times we blame God for it, yet it is possessing it that makes us human and gives us a share in the Divine Nature. It is this, with all its attendant qualities of reason, self-awareness, and love, that makes us creatures formed in the image and likeness of God.

CHAPTER TWELVE

PARADISE LOST

FINDING SOMEONE TO BLAME

e cannot speak of moral evil without sooner or later saying something about the origin of it. Theodicies are taken up not only with their attempt to explain the nature of wrong, but to show how sin entered the world in the first place. Granted our free will, how did we come to misuse it so grievously and thereby fall so lamentably?

I find the question mystifying. How could we ever imagine that we would not misuse our freedom? If we think of created beings, in possession of themselves, equipped with reason, placed at sufficient distance from their Creator to be able to assert their own will and inclinations, with their roots in their animal nature, subject to the temptation of being able at any moment to declare their independence of their Creator, and with God's permission to do anything except the one thing alone that they were forbidden to do, how would they not yield to temptation and fall into sin? The astonishing thing is not that there was a Fall, but that we could ever think that there would not be!

There is little mystery about it, then. As soon as Eden is set up, and Adam and Eve occupy the Garden, we know that the Fall is going to happen. It should not take us by surprise when it does, and we should not think that God was astonished by it, as though the possibility of its happening had never occurred to Him. Why are we sometimes so silly as to imagine that God isn't very smart?

THE NATURE OF MYTH

All this would, I think, be more immediately obvious to us if we did not so seriously misunderstand the nature of the magnificent myth of original sin and the Fall that is told us in Genesis. Myths are misunderstood in two ways. Some think of them as lies. They refer to them, and dismiss them contemptuously, as falsehoods. Others misunderstand the nature of myths by equating them with historical facts. They think that for the myth to have meaning, it must have happened; the story it tells must be grounded in an actual historical event or events. By these misunderstandings of their nature, myths are either to be dismissed as false or taken as history.

What both views fail to understand is how the poetic imagination, quickened by faith, can show us the meaning of things without having to make them bits of history to do so. Truths do not need to be factually and literally true before they can be the bearers of meaning. It is our failure to understand this that once led Reinhold Niebuhr to wonder how an age that is so devoid of poetic imagination as ours can be truly religious.

IS ANY SIN ORIGINAL?

Myths do not inform us of something that once happened; they describe something that happens all the time. History may invite us to look back, but myths invite us to look in. It was by looking in, and by trying to express what they found there, that men created them in the first place. To prove the truth of the Fall we do not send archaeologists off with spades to dig for history; we invite them to find all the evidence they will ever need by doing a little digging in their own nature.

It is not just the Paradise of Eden that has been lost; we all can remember paradises that we knew. We ourselves are aware of a lost innocence, a lost purity, and a lost content. We are certain that all men are wicked, not only because the story of Eden tells us that they are, but because we know ourselves to be wicked. If we are aware that we are fallen creatures, it is not because Eve was tempted and fell, but because her experience is for us a daily occurrence. Why, the Fall may be empirically proven any old morning by the simple act of buying a daily newspaper.

The value of myths is that they invite us, not only to see what they show us, but to make what they show us our way of seeing. This is how the dogma of original sin, for example, becomes, not something that once happened, but a way of seeing everything that happens and of interpreting everything we see. The Fall is not an event; it is the awareness that nothing is as it should be; it is the perception that the evil in the world is pervasive, universal, and intractable. We may say of myths what Father Owen Lee so splendidly says of legends: "Everything about a legend, save the literal facts, is true."

"THE DEVIL MADE ME DO IT"

Many have attempted to explain the origin of evil by blaming it on the Devil. He is accused of bringing it into the world as part of the trappings and mind-set of a fallen angel.

Now, we have already noticed that one of the benefits of this explanation is to remind us that the world is not evil, but fallen, that goodness is always prior to wickedness. Evils are not discrete entities, but good things gone wrong. For this reason, the Devil must be an angel to begin with, because he could not exist apart from the excellence against which he rebelled and his continuing tenuous connection with it.

Yet as explanations go, this particular explanation does not go very far. Those who cannot understand how we could ever have fallen by turning from the Paradise of Eden will surely find it even more difficult to explain how an angel could ever have spurned the Paradise of Heaven. When we try to blame the

Devil for the coming of evil into the world, we simply move the question one stage further back and make the explanation even more remote and implausible.

There is another sense in which the Devil is not helpful in our attempt to understand the presence and nature of wickedness. It is that the psychology of both angels and demons is further removed from us than psychology of a human kind. If I do not understand my own perverseness, how can I think to shed light on it by attempting to understand the perverseness of Satan? If, having personal access to it, I cannot understand my own mind on this matter, how on earth can I hope to comprehend it by attempting to interpret the mind of the Devil? Besides, being the Devil, he would surely refuse to help by allowing me to discover the secrets of any of his thoughts, devices, or stratagems. (It is characteristic of devils to feel themselves under no obligation to help us understand anything, least of all themselves.)

THINKING DEVILISHLY

It is not that we find the Devil helpful in explaining ourselves; it is our insight into ourselves that enables us to understand the Devil. As I mentioned earlier, when C. S. Lewis was writing his *Screwtape Letters*, he came to hate the book because to write it he had to think like the Devil. I mean, literally so. It was not simply that he had to think very hard, or that the Devil coached him in what to say; he had to tell the Devil what to say, and to do so had to think satanically—that is, perversely and wickedly—about everything. The Devil does not help us to understand ourselves; rather, it is by knowing ourselves that we understand the Devil.

Years ago Flip Wilson had a skit in which his "Geraldine" went off and bought herself an expensive dress. When she later modeled the garment, she was told that when tempted to buy it she should have resisted the temptation by saying, "Get thee behind me, Satan!" To which Geraldine replied, "That is what I did say, and the Devil told me it looked very nice from the back."

Isn't it astonishing that Satan so often sounds exactly like us? The Devil does not tell us what to say, or interpret us to ourselves; we put words in his mouth and make him the voice of our own desires. We treat the Devil as I am sometimes treated by those who come, ostensibly to ask my advice, but actually to have me approve what they have already decided. All they are really interested in hearing is what they wish to hear. They take my voice and make it an echo of their own.

ON NOT BLAMING EVE

The commonest explanation of the origin of moral evil is to blame it on Eve. She was the first to sin, and not only sinned herself, but taught her "husband" to sin, and through him led the whole world astray. Sin and death thus found entry into paradise. The first sin was Eve's disobedience when she plucked and ate the forbidden fruit. As she herself explained when she attempted to excuse what she had done, "The serpent beguiled me, and I did eat."

Yet if she did not initiate the first offense, but was in fact "beguiled" at the beginning, it suggests that the beginning itself must have been something less than perfect. It tells us that the first sin was not the disobedience of Eve and Adam, but the serpent's lie. For the snake repudiated the divine warning that they should neither touch nor eat the fruit of the forbidden tree lest they die, with his own, "Ye shall not surely die." Eve was deceived by the serpent's big fib; her disobedience was the success of Satan's lie.

"RESPECT FOR THE WORD"

Historian Paul Johnson once said that lying is the foreword to the encyclopedia of evil, and so it would appear to be here. Eve's world was already an imperfect world before she went anywhere near the forbidden fruit. Hammarskjøld was right: to misuse the word is to show contempt for man, it is to undermine the bridges and poison the wells. Or, to put it another way, it is paradise lost.

The Fall is carried back to Eve because of what she represents; and what she represents in the story of the Fall is what women have always represented in mythical settings: She is that part of the psyche of each of us that is profoundly intuitive and venturesome, that emerges from the savage and beautiful country of the unconscious and is of the deepest sensibility.

This frequently places us in harm's way and is the occasion of much anguish and distress. Yet it invariably moves things forward by testing the limits of knowledge and pressing the margins of perception. It thereby raises us to new levels of awareness and discernment and is, ultimately, the gift of hope. That is why the sin of Eve is also the *felix culpa,* the "happy fault" that brought upon us, not only all the sorrows of the world, but that incomparable and inexpressible rush of grace that was the coming of Jesus into the world. It was Eve's sin that brought to us "the Second Adam," our "Champion in the field" who "to the fight and to the rescue came."

"THE MANY FACES OF EVE"

Those unfamiliar with the Jewish and Christian faiths might wonder what has been going on in this chapter. Are they really expected to tune out the modern world and tune in the world we have described, which has a distinctly medieval, if not ancient, flavor about it? What sense are they to make of forbidden fruit, a tree of the knowledge of good and evil, a talking snake taken by some to be the Devil in disguise, and a Fall? It is all very strange and alien to their way of thinking. They want to know if we really expect them to take it all seriously. Their incredulity can make them a bit uppity about it, too.

Well, to answer their question: we do indeed mean them to take it seriously, though we do not mean them to take it literally. And they really oughtn't to become the least bit uppity about it for, as the Irish would say, "They haven't heard the half of it!" We have a few more stories for them that are not quite as good as the one we have been discussing, but have nevertheless informed the consciousness of all of us and have created and shaped the most basic presuppositions and ways of perceiving of Western civilization. The Genesis myth of the Fall is the most important of a great number of myths that have substantial things to say to us about our own nature, about the nature of the world, and about the nature of the evils that are in the world. Whether we think ourselves modern or medieval makes no difference at all.

EVE GOES TO THE OPERA

I watched the Fall played out before my eyes a couple of weeks ago in a performance of Wagner's *Lohengrin* at the Metropolitan Opera. It was not only seen and said, but played splendidly by Jimmy Levine's orchestra and gloriously sung by Ben Heppner and Karita Mattila and every member of the cast and chorus.

Eve is now Elsa of Brabant, championed by a mysterious stranger with whom she falls in love and who loves her. If you had "Here Comes the Bride" played at your wedding, it was their wedding music you borrowed. Elsa does not know the name of her beloved husband; for he has warned her, not once only, but twice, and with the utmost deliberation and clarity, that if she asks his name, or where he is from, their bliss will end. Ortrude and her husband Telramund, who play the part played by the snake in Eden, sow the seeds of discontent in Elsa, so that she finally asks her lover the forbidden question.

The sadness is now overwhelming. Elsa stands stricken while the man she adores tells his name and reveals his heritage to her, and to the king and the assembled company, before departing forever. He is Lohengrin, son of Parsifal, Knight of the Grail. But by her doing what he had asked her not to do, all joy is forfeited. She will not see him again; as Shakespeare would say, "Never, never, never, never, never." It is Paradise Lost. It is the Fall. It is all good and great things freely given and tragically lost by snatching at the one small thing withheld.

THE IMPORTANCE OF KEEPING THE LID ON

So much for Eve as Elsa of Brabant; but she has other names. She is also Semele, a mortal woman loved by Zeus, king of the Olympian gods, who asks of her only that she not ask to see his glory. She does ask, and sees, of course, and perishes by looking. Eve is also Psyche, who is allowed to touch but not to look on Cupid, her lover. Nevertheless she lights a lamp and gazes on him. But when a spot of hot oil touches and awakens him, he goes off into the darkness, leaving her desolate. And Eve is Pandora, the all-giving first woman, fashioned from the earth and entrusted with a box of evils she is forbidden to open. Open it she does, though, and spills all the miseries of the world all over the earth.

We must not think, then, that the Genesis story of Adam and Eve and the Garden of Eden and the serpent and the forbidden fruit and the Fall is strange and unusual. The great myths of our culture and tradition try to tell us some of the same truths without managing to do it quite so well. There are important differences between the myths, but most of the great motifs are in place in all of them.

GRIMM STORIES

We may find the same themes in less ancient and exalted places. Chesterton found some of them in *Grimm's Fairy Tales.*

Indeed, in "The Ethics of Elfland," a chapter of his *Orthodoxy,* he took and made them into a doctrine that he calls "the doctrine of conditional joy." It states explicitly the truth we learned in the nursery without being aware that we were learning it: that all joy hangs on a veto and that the word "if" is the most important word in the moral vocabulary of fairyland.

The meaning of conditional joy is that our enjoyment of all the wondrous, colossal, dizzy, wild, and whirling things that are given to us depends on one small thing that is withheld from us or forbidden to us. We may marry the king's daughter, or live in a palace of gold, so long as we don't show the young lady an onion or say the word "cow." We may ride off to the ball in a fairy coach from somewhere and with a coachman who appears from nowhere, but we had better be home by twelve.

Chesterton tells us that, from the beginning, our happiness depended on our not doing something we could at any moment do, and which, very often, it was not obvious why we should not do it. In elfland and in life, "an incomprehensible happiness rests upon an incomprehensible condition."

Yet we are not deprived or cheated by this. If Cinderella were to complain, "Why should there be a curfew?" the answer is another question, "Why should there be a ball?" It is God's answer to Job out of the whirlwind and to Eve in the Garden of Eden. Eve, then, may also be called Cinderella, for they learned the same truth and share it with us for our benefit.

Robert Frost used to say that writing free verse is like playing tennis with the net down. He reminds us that if we don't play by the rules of the game then there isn't any game. If we take away the net we do not make tennis easier, we make tennis impossible. Rules are not the enemy of freedom; they make it possible.

CHAPTER THIRTEEN

I'M OK—
YOU'RE OK?

"THE MORNING AFTER OPTIMISM"

*T*here is, of course, an "I'm OK—You're OK" view of our nature and the world that will give short shrift to everything we have written about sin and evil. It refuses to recognize moral wrongdoing, or evil of any kind. Here we have the three little monkeys who seem to think that if only they see no evil, speak no evil, and hear no evil, there will be no evil. It is the old trinity of unawareness freshened up with a little spit-and-polish from pop psychology. How naively they underestimate our capacity for mischief, and how grossly they overestimate the content of our character!

Not many years ago, grown men and women stood in front of their morning mirror, looked their drowsy reflection more or less straight in the eye, and attempted to convince themselves that every day in every way they were getting better and better. How did they manage to keep a straight face? Why did their sense of humor not break in to save them from their silliness? It didn't though; so undeterred, and with a little help from Darwin, they persuaded themselves that everything was on the up-and-up, inevitably, irresistibly, everywhere, and all the time.

We had thought that all such fantasies of human perfectibility perished in the Holocaust and the Gulag, that we had learned from experience that evil is universal, pervasive, and intractable. But old heresies never die and seldom fade away. They just assume another form.

Some churches, even, fearful that any mention of imperfection might offend the unfaithful, decided never to bring the matter up. They called the weekly confession of sin a "downer" and dispensed with it from public worship. They thinned out their gospel until, as one theologian said, it became the story of how "a God without wrath, brings men without sin, into a Kingdom without judgment, through the ministrations of a Christ without a cross." Cheerful worship ended, home the happy parishioners went, equipped with the power of positive thinking to pursue their perfect ends by perfect means in the best of all possible worlds.

How like dear Walt Whitman they were, who thought he might go and live with the animals because they do not lie awake in the dark and weep for their sins. He didn't, though; for the animals who do not confess their sins do not read his poetry either. Being animals, they're not big on either penitence or literary appreciation. Our *mea culpa,* far from giving us reason to join them, raised us a cut above them; for it reminded us that we are responsible creatures who have not only lost our innocence, but live in a world of moral expectation and moral failure.

"Something Wicked This Way Comes"

Thank God for the editors, dramatists, poets, and novelists who kept their wits about them and saw through this nonsense—for Richard Crossman, for example, who thought that the state of the world said more for the doctrine of original sin than for Rousseau's idea of the Noble Savage, the Noble Savage having proved more savage than noble.

Ogden Nash told us that progress was a good idea once, but has been going on too long. Edna St. Vincent Millay called it the dirtiest word in the language for it has come to mean impetus without direction, rather like running in the dark.

Dublin's Abbey Theater produced a play called *The Morning*

After Optimism while Sam Pekinpah defended the violence of his movies by warning us that to ignore our dark side is to become the victim of it. Eugene O'Neill skewered optimism of the American sort in *The Iceman Cometh*, and Arthur Miller echoed it in *Death of a Salesman*.

Matthew Arnold spoke of "the something that infects the world," and Flannery O'Connor wrote a chilling short story and called it, "A Good Man Is Hard to Find." When a reader complained that it had left a bad taste in her mouth, O'Connor replied unsympathetically that she hadn't intended she should eat it. Ray Bradbury borrowed words from Macbeth's witches to share his own premonition that *Something Wicked This Way Comes,* while Spalding Gray sold out a New York theater by talking about evil, describing it as a cloud that moves over the face of the earth settling here and there now and then. Yesterday in Germany; today in Cambodia; and tomorrow, who knows?

Lord of the Flies set up another Eden and described another Fall, this time among the junior members of the race; and in *Those Blue Remembered Hills* Dennis Potter echoed the message on television to make sure we hadn't missed it.

But Yeats, in his greatest poem, was better than any of them; for he saw things fall apart, and innocence drowned in a blood-red tide, and anarchy loosed upon the world. And in the sands of the desert, a beast with the body of a lion and the head of a man, with a gaze blank and pitiless, stirred itself, moved its slow thighs, and slouched towards Bethlehem to birth a new age of horror and destruction.

WHAT THE RABBI SAID TO THE PSYCHOLOGIST

There is yet another view of the evil we have described. I encountered it as lately as this morning as I sat in my dentist's waiting room reading his copy of *Reader's Digest*. In one of the articles, a rabbi expressed his disagreement with the modern attitude toward those who do evil things. His complaint was that we have come to regard moral failure as though it were nothing more than a problem for psychology. When someone does wrong, we do not any longer send for the priest to minister to a sinner, we find a psychologist to counsel a patient. We do not say that the wrongdoer is evil, we say that person is ill. What such a person needs is not absolution, but therapy. Our duty is to understand, not blame.

Now there is obviously something to be said for this view of bad conduct. It is spontaneously expressed in our reaction to news of behavior that is cruel and senseless. We simply say of the person who is guilty of it, "He's sick!" We acknowledge in this way that whatever else the evil attitudes and actions are, they are certainly not wellness; and we ought to be grateful for any light or help the psychiatrist may be able to offer in dealing with deeds of such an unhappy and unhealthy sort.

Yet the rabbi has a point, too. Sin may not be health, yet it is something other and more than illness. About some aspects of its nature the psychiatrist can have little to say; and this will be true, not because the priest wishes to defend his professional turf, but because the definition of sin is not a psychological definition, but a theological one. Sin is wrongdoing in its relation to God. It is the discrepancy between what we are and what God wishes us to be. Here it is, perfectly expressed in a Hebridean prayer:

Take me often from the tumult of things into Thy Presence. There show me what I am, and what Thou hast purposed me to be. Then hide me from Thy tears.

Is it, then, the psychologist's work to either affirm or deny the divine intention, and pronounce judgment on what God has purposed us to be?

What the Psychologist Tells the Preacher

When I mention these matters to my friends who are psychologists, they tell me that if they are to be helpful to those who come to see them, they must have some idea, not only of the sort of person it is who is seeking their help, but also of the kind of person they would like to be. "Tell me who you are and what you wish to become," they tell their patients, and go forward from there.

Now, if those who have sought their help are persons of faith, then their belief in God and their awareness of His purposes will be a vital part of their sense of self, both of the self they are and of the self they wish to become. A skillful therapist will be able to suggest ways that will help them fulfill, and will warn of dangers that would keep them from realizing, their best hopes. But surely it is no function of the psychiatrist to decide what those hopes should be.

Who Decides What? and How?

There is a modern tendency to define too narrowly the perplexing personal and social issues we must make up our minds about and to limit those who will decide the issue to one particular segment of our society. In this way, the issue of abortion, for example, is sometimes made into a woman's issue to be decided by one gender. But abortion is not an issue for women to decide, though women will have much to contribute to the continuing debate concerning it. Abortion is a moral issue that demands the deepest consideration by all thoughtful people, whatever their gender.

The same may be said of the debate about euthanasia and assisted suicide. There are those who assume that the decisions to be made about it are purely medical decisions. It is the physician who will determine the "quality of life" of the person and will then decide if and when a particular life should be ended. But this is to place an intolerable burden on the physician, and it is to relinquish our own responsibility to understand and decide the issue.

The question of whether it is permissible for us to end another person's life is not a medical question at all. It is a moral question that requires the best thought, not only of physicians, but of all wise and thoughtful people, in deciding it. Once again, Chesterton gets it exactly right. In an essay on "Science and Religion" he writes, "I want my private physician to tell me whether this or that food will kill me. It is for my private philosopher to tell me whether I ought to be killed."

The truth is that I'm not OK, and I don't think you are either, and I am certain that our world is not. Yet far from this being a depressing thought, it is the only cheerful one. If there is something wrong with us, it means that there is something about us that might be put right. But if the present state of things is to be accepted as normal, proper, and fitting, then what better prospect is left to us? If we will not acknowledge a Paradise Lost, how can we hope for Paradise Regained?

CHAPTER FOURTEEN

"IT'S IN THE BOOK!"

"THINGS HAVE THEIR TEARS"

*I*t may help us to remember that our question is not new, but is as old as time, and as deep as life, and has found expression, in one form or other, in the best poetry, drama, music, and art of our culture. One of the most eloquent expressions of it is Virgil's *Aeneid,* which is among the most beautiful, poignant, and civilizing achievements of the human spirit. In it, Virgil remembers, feels, foresees, and laments the fallenness of our nature, the ambiguity of all things human, and the tragedy of our kind. As he sings "of arms and the man" he grieves that power is so seldom the instrument of love and so frequently the bringer of wars, both civil and foreign; that to fulfill a noble destiny is often the occasion of ignoble suffering; that our greatness is inseparable from our failure, our splendor from our tragedy, our joy from our sorrow. He wonders why peace is so seldom achieved without a call to arms; why the world is so full of chaotic energies and mindless anguish; why the rebirth of Troy in the birth of Rome is accomplished by Aeneas, the last Trojan and first Roman, only at the cost of unbearable pain, not only to those who oppose him and wish him harm, but to those who love him, the offspring of his loins and the woman who holds him as her heart's dear treasure.

Virgil was right:

And look,
Priam! Even here glory her laurel wears:
Here mortal fates are felt: things have their tears.

Indeed they have, yet there are never tears enough for all the things that cause them. The tears, says Virgil, are always *inanes,* that is, insufficient.

THE IMPATIENCE OF JOB

The same matters are up for debate when we journey from "the topless towers of Ilium" and "the walls of Troy, famed in battle," to the land of Uz, better known as Edom. This is the country in which the events and speeches recounted in the book of Job are set by a sublime poet who, perhaps as much as five hundred years before Virgil, asked why God afflicts the innocent.

Virgil's questions, and others besides, are asked again, but with a different twist and in a different setting. The *Aeneid* is panoramic; its action sweeps us to, from, and beyond Troy, Carthage, and Italy. The book of Job is about one righteous, prosperous man, his family and his friends, and the disasters that came upon him. Yet such is the skill of the poet that this local and domestic drama is infused with cosmic significance. What is at risk is not merely the innocence of Job, but the honor of God.

"JUST ONE DAMNED THING AFTER ANOTHER"

Job's suffering is of every sort and leaves no energy for anything save the bearing of it. Here, in one person, are all the slings and arrows of outrageous fortune and all the ills that flesh is heir to.

The drama begins by showing us a just, kind, and happy

man of substance. No doubt the lines have fallen unto him in pleasant places, but his wealth has been the instrument of his compassion and his prosperity the occasion of much good.

Suddenly, everything changes. His flocks and herds are stolen by rustlers, and his servants murdered. A whirlwind shatters the house in which his children are having a party and all are killed. One disaster follows upon another with bewildering speed. Finally, Job's own flesh erupts in loathsome, running sores. He now spends his sleepless nights and wakeful days in physical pain, mental distress, and spiritual anguish.

His questions now come as fast as his afflictions: Why has God turned against him? Is God pleased that his servant is mocked by those who once revered him that his integrity has been questioned and his dignity assaulted? Why this disastrous change in fortune? He knows he has done nothing to deserve it; why, then, has it come upon him? His wife thinks there is nothing left but to "curse God and die," thus inviting her husband to add to his other losses a loss of faith.

"THE FIRST DISSIDENT"

Job will have none of it. To accept his wife's suggestion would mean surrendering the two convictions that not only puzzle and torment him, but define and sustain his very self. For Job is convinced both of his own innocence and of the kindness of God.

This trustfulness does not express itself in a meek, unquestioning submission to the injustice that plagues him or a resigning of himself to the mystery of it. Job is furious. He utters his faith in anger and voices it in a rage. His fierce indignation not only lacerates his heart but inspires a godly irreverence towards God and a storming impatience with conventional pieties. For Job is a desperate man who does not know himself apart from faith and whose life means nothing to him if drained of devotion and emptied of integrity.

THE STIGMA OF DOGMA

Nor does Job assent to ancient orthodoxies, however hallowed by age or cherished by tradition, when they appear vacuous. His insistence on his own innocence and the divine justice, however mild it seems to us in our time, was explosive in his own. For it challenged the Deuteronomist, who maintained that the good are unfailingly rewarded with length of days and temporal blessings while the wicked are invariably punished by material loss and an early grave. God's justice saw to it.

All this is more than Job can bear. It is distressing enough that he has lost everything; to be told that his predicament can be explained by his wickedness and solved by his penitence is outrageous; it is far too much to take without a moral, intellectual, and spiritual reaction. That the innocent suffer he can demonstrate from his own integrity and his own wounds. He knows himself to be, and is known to be, a good man; yet look at his skin coming off and his children in their graves before their father! Little wonder William Safire designates Job "the first dissident."

WITH FRIENDS LIKE THESE

Things take a turn for the worse when several of Job's friends, having learned of his troubles, arrive to comfort him. They get off to a pretty good start. Shocked at the severity of his condition and subdued by the greatness of his suffering, they have enough sense to sit on the ground for a while and hold their tongues.

But not for long, for they cannot resist the temptation to offer advice, and soon begin to mouth the clichés of thoughtless

piety and the platitudes of conventional belief. God is just; only
the wicked suffer; if Job were blameless these things would not
happen to him; he must repent forthwith and await the restora-
tion of his good fortune.

His friends have become an added affliction. They possess an
inexhaustible supply of pious platitudes, which they deliver
with sanctimonious pomposity. So puffed up are they that they
talk down to him with spurious arguments he has already
spurned. He says they are an appalling assortment of old wind-
bags; "miserable comforters are you all," he tells them.

ON NOT TURNING UP FOR A SHOWDOWN

What Job really wants is a chance to make his case before
God, to come into the divine presence armed with argument,
hot with indignation, sure of the rightness of his complaint, and
demanding an answer. He wants to stand in front of his Maker
and look Him in the eye and hear the divine explanation; yet it
appears that when God is most needed He is most absent. Job's
desire is what the ancient Irish would call *aisling,* which means
the longing for an absence, for the Almighty is nowhere to be
found. It adds bitterness to Job's torment and insults his complaint that when he cries out the cold heaven makes no reply.
The only answer is silence and the echo of the absence of God.

What is he left with? He is certain that there is more of God
in his own irreverence than there is in his friends' obsequious
piety. It is then that Job utters his sublime persuasion that if
God is not just, then He is not God. The Almighty's faithful
servant has come to the defense of the divine honor, for what
Job maintains is that God cannot be as careless as He seems. If
He is, then Job will appeal to the God behind God, the true
God, who will plead his cause, champion his innocence, and
vindicate his integrity, though he go to his grave unjustified.

If we think Job impious in going behind God's back to find

his Champion, then we should remember that he is doing only what we do when we ask God to save us from "acts of God." And Job had more and better reasons to do so than we have. Robert Frost, in "A Masque of Reason," captures perfectly the spirit of this "first dissident." God speaks His gratitude to His good servant who has helped Him to establish once and for all that

> There's no connection man can reason out
> Between his just deserts and what he gets.

WHY JOB'S COMFORTERS WERE MISERABLE

How and why did Job's friends let him down? They were miserable comforters because they failed to comfort. And their failure was for two reasons. The first is that they allowed their need to explain the suffering to freeze their pity for the sufferer. So eager were they to admonish that they failed to be kind. Addressing the question, they missed the person. They thought it more important to set Job straight than to imagine what it must be like to go through what he was going through. They did not offer their friend the solace of tenderness, or steady him by their trust, or sustain him by their faithfulness. They confronted, blamed, and rebuked him for what they judged to be his moral failure. And then, having behaved with such appalling insensitivity, they presumed themselves sensitive enough to explain the suffering they had failed to feel. No wonder Job lost all confidence in them, all respect for them, and all patience with them. Things may have their tears, but none of them were shed by the friends of Job.

IF IT DOESN'T KILL YOU

Second, Job's comforters failed after another fashion when they thought they would do their friend good by telling him that his troubles were good for him. Good for him? But Job had not needed his troubles to make him good. What good could there be in the loss of his prosperity, the destruction of his family, and the rotting of his own flesh when he had been a good man before any of these things happened? Undiscouraged, his friends lied about that, too. Job was not innocent, as he thought, for the innocent do not suffer; only the guilty do. Job's suffering therefore declares his guilt.

That the innocent suffer, Job has learned from his own experience. He has both the virtue and the scars to prove it. And knowing it in his own conscience and feeling it in his own flesh enables him to discern the fact of it everywhere. How can his comforters fail to acknowledge this when the proof of it is everywhere displayed? To feel the force of it, all they need do is open their eyes and discover their hearts. Instead, they deny the facts to preserve a dogma and sacrifice their friend to a false theory.

BEEN THERE, DONE THAT?

Like Job, we blame his comforters; but not because we have suffered as he did. We censure them because, having attempted to do what they did, we know firsthand why they failed. We dislike them because they remind us of ourselves. Their blunders are all too familiar from our having repeated them. When confronted by another's woe, we too rated the value of the instruction we wished to deliver more highly than the love we might have shown. We allowed our conceit to blind us to what was happening in front of our eyes. How testy we grew when our arguments did not immediately persuade and our insights convince! How offended we were when our advice gave more offense than comfort! We were little better than the insurance agent who wants to sell us a policy, not for our security, but for the commission. We failed, not only from a dearth of wisdom, but from our lack of humility and want of love. Like Job's friends, we were in it for us, not for him. We might

have learned better from Blake the nature of comfort, our own and
God's:

> Can I see another's woe,
> And not be in sorrow too?
> Can I see another's grief,
> And not seek for kind relief?
>
> Can I see a falling tear,
> And not feel my sorrow's share?
> Can a father see his child
> Weep, nor be with sorrow fill'd?
>
> Can a mother sit and hear
> An infant groan an infant fear?
> No, no! never can it be!
> Never, never can it be!
>
> O He gives to us His joy
> That our grief He may destroy;
> Till our grief is fled and gone
> He doth sit by us and moan.

LONG AGO AND FAR AWAY?

If Job seems long ago and far away, it is not because he is so
out of date that we have left him behind, but because he is so
far in front of us that we have not yet caught up with him. We
have not listened to him or taken his words to heart. It is as
though he had never lived or suffered or spoken, for we have not
believed him. And his friends are with us still. Let me prove it
to you.

A couple of years ago, when heavy rains flooded the
Midwest, washing away homes and sweeping people to their
death, eighteen out of every hundred Americans thought that

the deluge was God's way of punishing the people of those states for their wickedness. Now, I have friends in the Midwest whom I have never considered more wicked than the friends I have in New York, though they may have fewer temptations. The same 18 percent of Americans would probably have said the same thing about the California earthquakes that occurred at about the same time as the floods.

As I write this, the current issue of *Newsweek* describes recent disasters in China by reporting:

> After a summer of Noah-like floods, China's Biblical chaos continues: now Xinjiang province is facing a plague of locusts.

Far more than 18 percent of us know the reason for *those* catastrophes: it is because the Chinese are "Godless communists," of course. But if that is the reason, what are we to make of similar floods in Texas, where they do everything in a big way and have some of the largest Christian churches in the world?

UNDER THE RAINBOW

It seems only natural that the story of Noah's flood should come up every time there is a natural disaster on a large scale. The trouble is that we remember the drowning of the world and forget the rainbow, which is a great pity, for the rainbow is the whole point of the story of Noah and the great flood. It is God's rainbow, and He hangs it above the earth as in olden days bowmen hung their war-bows on the wall when they returned from war. Hanging up the bow meant that the war was over; conflict was at an end. So, too, the rainbow is the arch of God's mercy; it is the divine sign and pledge that, at least on His side, there is no enmity between Him and us. Listen to the book of Genesis:

I do set my bow in the cloud, and it shall be for a token of a covenant between me and the earth. And it shall come to pass, when I bring a cloud over the earth, that the bow shall be seen in the cloud: And I will remember my covenant, which is between me and you and every living creature of all flesh; and the waters shall no more become a flood to destroy all flesh. And the bow shall be in the cloud; and I will look upon it that I may remember the everlasting covenant between God and every living creature of all flesh that is upon the earth. (KJV)

"YOUR GOD IS MY DEVIL!"

I knew a young woman who on one occasion slept with a man who was not her husband. A year later she became ill and was told by her physician that she had cancer. When she came to see me I assumed, naturally enough, that she wanted to talk to me about her illness; but I was wrong. She said having cancer was no fun, but she thought she was coping pretty well. What she wanted to talk about was not the disease, but the reaction of some of her religious friends when they learned she had it. They adopted an attitude of enormous moral superiority and told her, with about as much grace as Job's friends exhibited when they charged him with wickedness, that God had afflicted her with cancer to punish her fornication.

She wanted to know from me if she should believe them, if that is how God treats those who stumble, sending major disasters to punish minor offenses? That the innocent suffer she had no doubt; but is God the kind of nasty old sod who runs the world by cruelty and terror, visiting dreadful afflictions on those who offend Him?

ONE CAUSE OF MS

When Jacqueline Du Pré, that superb cellist, fell madly in love and married the man she adored, she surrendered what had been a nominal Christianity to embrace the faith of her husband, who was Jewish. A few years later, the first signs of the multiple sclerosis that was to end her career, and then her life, appeared. She bore her illness with grace, humor, and a wholesome earthiness that enabled her to talk about her body as though it belonged to someone else, thus saving her much embarrassment.

One of the hardest things she had to put up with was that two of the people closest to her, one of them her fundamentalist Christian mother, told her that God had afflicted her with MS because she had turned from Christian faith and had become Jewish. Her rabbi and she had become firm friends, however, and responded to her mother's explanation by saying that now they knew at least *one* of the causes of MS.

William Barclay was a biblical scholar whose writings have been enormously helpful to both ministers and laity for over sixty years. One bright summer afternoon his daughter and son-in-law, on holiday in Ireland, went sailing off the coast of County Antrim, but perished in a sudden squall that blew up. Soon after, Professor Barclay received an anonymous letter telling him that God had drowned his daughter and her husband to get even with him for his heretical teaching. The letter, being anonymous, was unanswerable; but Dr. Barclay said that if he had been able to do so, he would have answered the writer in the words of John Wesley: "Your God is my devil!"

If natural disasters and painful illness are God's way of punishing the wicked for their wickedness, how is it that so many of us have escaped? Should we conclude that in the judgment of God we are the virtuous ones? The thought makes me nervous, for one of the reiterated messages of scripture is that the righteous are seldom those who think they are. Those whose conceit has usurped their compassion are surely not among them.

VERILY, VERILY, NOW HEAR THIS!

Of course, it might be simpler to listen to the words of Jesus on this matter, for no one ever spoke more plainly about it than He did:

> There were present at that season some that told him of the Galileans, whose blood Pilate had mingled with their sacrifices. And Jesus answering said unto them, Suppose ye that these Galileans were sinners above all the Galileans, because they suffered such things? I tell you, Nay . . . Or those eighteen, upon whom the tower in Siloam fell, and slew them, think ye that they were sinners above all men that dwelt in Jerusalem? I tell you, Nay. (KJV)

On another occasion He speaks of God's indiscriminate goodness by telling us that our Heavenly Father makes His sun to shine on the righteous and the unrighteous, and sends His rain on good and bad alike. Why is it that when He has made it so plain, we do not believe what He tells us and stop, once and for all, our often prejudiced, petty, and silly chatter about whether or not the innocent and guilty get what they deserve? We should be thankful that, in the kindness of God, none of us gets what we deserve. D. J. Enright ends a splendid poem on the prosperity of the wicked with the comment:

> Though there's no justice in the world,
> There's an injustice that can work as well.

What a strange idea it is to think of envying the wicked! It is as though, for all our praise of virtue, we really believed that good people get the short end of the stick.

The Stoics were wiser than that. Epictetus exhorts us not to covet what others have if we are not prepared to do what they were willing to do to get it. We should not envy the prosperity of the wicked if we are not willing to behave wickedly to obtain it.

Surely we do what is right, not because it will prosper us, but because it is right; and we do good, not because it will increase our wealth or improve our health, but because we love goodness. If we are honest, it must not be because honesty is the best policy, but because honesty is honest! When goodness becomes a matter of policy, a mere stratagem, its virtue is suspect and its quality forfeited.

CHAPTER FIFTEEN

THE
COMPANY
OF
DISSIDENTS

"EVIL HAS COME, THOUGH I EXPECTED GOOD"

Virgil and Job are two of the great ones of the ancient world, who, from different parts of it and at different times, were not only forthright but eloquent in their description and questioning of the Divine ordering of things. Others were soon to take up their complaints and further refine and elevate what they had dared to say about the justice and honor of God.

The writer of the Seventy-third Psalm, for example, shares with us the personal disappointment that brought him almost to despair when he considered how badly God had treated him. To begin with, he had thought himself virtuous enough to deserve something extra, some over-and-above benefit to acknowledge and reward his better-than-average probity. He proceeded, therefore, in William James's fine phrase, "to lobby for special favors in the courts of the Almighty."

When he did not receive any, he dutifully cut his cloth to suit his garment and reduced his expectation to one of simple justice. He no longer looked for special favors; fairness alone would suffice, a nicely calculated tit-for-tat arrangement by which the good should be rewarded in proportion to their goodness and the evil punished as their wickedness deserved.

This seemed to the psalmist a modest-enough proposal; yet even this weakened hope was not honored. To add insult to injury, it seemed to him that the wicked enjoyed all the advantages, received all the special favors, and were not above making fun of the righteous and mocking their God.

The psalmist couldn't work it out. When he went into the Temple and tried to make sense of it, he decided he was working on too short a timeline and that the wicked would get their comeuppance in the end. It was a great idea, but it needed a little work. And the author of the book of Daniel was just the one to do it.

"The Thing I Feared Is Come Upon Me"

What are we to make of the stories of Daniel and his companions, who because of their faithfulness to God and their unwillingness to bow their knee to the golden image set up by King Nebuchadnezzar on the plain of Dura, were thrown into a burning fiery furnace and a den of lions? The flames did not scorch them, and the lions did not bite, so that the faithful young men escaped with life and limb; and what are we to make of that?

We judge the stories fit for infants, the stuff of childhood's fantasy, but should think it silly to believe that there is anything in them we could count on. "Trust God, and He will rescue you," is Daniel's moral; and his stories of deliverance from death and danger are unforgettable examples of it. But experience is against them, for that is not how such affairs usually turn out. We are certain of this because we know many good people who trusted and were not delivered.

"All at Sea"

I remember reading an article by Chaplain Stephen Webster who was in Europe with the American forces during the Second

World War. It was an angry article called, "Who Gets the Breaks in Prayer?" The Chaplain told his readers that he was fed up with the stories of miraculous rescues at sea and deliverances from rafts adrift in the North Atlantic. The deliverances were often attributed by the faithful to the faith of the delivered, young men and women whose prayers were answered and whose trust in God, like Daniel's, was not put to shame, but vindicated, so that it accomplished their recovery and achieved their safe return to friends and family.

For his part, Chaplain Webster wished to honor the gallantry and faith of those who, unlike Daniel and his colleagues, trusted and were not saved, prayed and were not delivered, but went down with their ship or were eaten by sharks or expired from hunger, thirst, and exposure in an open boat. We cannot quite believe Daniel's edifying tales, for we know too many who trusted, and trustfully perished.

Oddly enough, so did Daniel. His stories seem strangely chosen and surprisingly told, for many who heard them were being thrust into the fire, and thrown to the lions, even as they listened. Daniel told his tales at a time when the troops of Antiochus Epiphanes, a madman who could have held his own with Hitler, Stalin, and all the thugs of history, were on a rampage. They seared, devoured, and slaughtered the faithful ones of Israel, who were not rescued, but massacred; and what did Daniel have to say about that?

WHAT DANIEL SAID

What Daniel had to say about it is what Daniel had already said: "Trust God and He will rescue you." But now their deliverance meant something it had never meant before. Now they would be saved from death, not by avoiding it, but by being brought through it. For the first time in the history of Israel's faith, Daniel declared the reality, substance, and consolation of immortal hope:

And many of them that sleep in the dust of the earth shall awake to everlasting life; and they that be wise shall shine as the brightness of the firmament; and they that turn many to righteousness as the stars for ever and ever.

An English poet who watched many die in the First World War put Daniel's promise in words of much beauty:

> Safe when all safety's lost,
> Safe where men fall.
> And if these poor limbs die,
> Safest of all.

RELIGION TRUE AND FALSE

John McMurray once expressed the difference between false religion and true by saying that the maxim of illusory religion runs, "Fear not! Trust in God and He will see that none of the things you fear will happen to you." The maxim of real religion, on the other hand, tells us: "Fear not! The things that you are afraid of are quite likely to happen to you, but they are nothing to be afraid of." One is reminded of what Vaclav Havel had to say about hope:

> It is not the conviction that something will turn out well, but the certainty that something makes sense regardless of how it turns out.

CHAPTER SIXTEEN

ON REFUSING
TO BE
A VICTIM

A QUALITY OF INNOCENCE

ou will have noticed that in our discussion so far we have talked about suffering as though it were something that happens to us. We really don't have much control over whether or not we become seriously ill, or suffer grief, or are crippled in an accident.

We take reasonable care, of course. We watch what we eat, and don't smoke, or drink to excess, and practice safe sex, and drive carefully, and take our vitamins, and exercise regularly. In these ways we do our best to hold illness off. This thoughtful, disciplined behavior permits us to hope that in its arbitrary comings and goings it will not come to us. Yet, for the most part, we are passive. Suffering is not anything we decide about, but something that may or may not afflict us. It is easy to feel, then, that we are helpless victims who can do little more than fear the worst and hope for the best. If suffering comes to us, we are quite likely to ask, "Why has this *happened* to me?"

Yet there are other ways of understanding suffering. The prophet Isaiah, for example, invites us to consider it in a different light and to engage it with a more active spirit. He thinks there is something better to be done with it than passively waiting for it to come and enduring it when it arrives. Isaiah sees it, not as something that happens to us, but as something that may be freely chosen and willingly embraced because we love God, adore another person, or hope to achieve a great good.

As soon as Isaiah says this, we feel that it must be true; and when we begin to think about it, we know that it is true. Freedom from pain is not our highest value, and avoiding suffering never was a program. We may sometimes choose danger, pain, and difficulty over security, ease, and pleasure in order to fulfill some desirable intention or fortify some quality we prize more highly than comfort. We may willingly assume a weight of suffering in order to protect others, defend our own integrity, serve our country, or rescue someone we love. This is what the French poet meant when he said that "whoever knows the meaning of love knows the meaning of death." Our martyrs and war casualties have proved it, and those who love prove it all the time.

"LET IT BE ME!"

Francis Bacon warns us, "He that hath wife and child hath given hostages to fortune." And those who love the hostages would happily pay their ransom if it were within their power to do so. A mother who loves her child will not only willingly, but eagerly, surrender her own life to save her little one.

Leslie Weatherhead once told of a group of archaeologists who discovered an Egyptian tomb containing a sarcophagus that enclosed the mummified figure of a little child. They opened it and read the inscribed words of the infant's mother, "Oh, my life, my love, my little one; would God I had died for thee!" I have heard the same words sobbed in an Irish farmhouse, and a Canadian hospital, and a Manhattan funeral home.

THE PROPHET OF ISRAEL AND
THE BELLE OF AMHERST

Isaiah goes even farther by thinking of death as he thinks of suffering. It need not be something that merely happens to us, but something we may accomplish. Emily Dickinson, the Belle of Amherst, has a shining sentence in which she speaks of "The overtakelessness of those who have *accomplished* death." There really is a difference between having our life taken from us and willingly laying it down for something or someone we love more than life.

It is in this way that Isaiah raises one of the most profound questions of life and faith. That the innocent suffer the prophet has no doubt; but what if their suffering has a particular quality and unique power *because* it is innocent? What would it mean if the innocent were to find themselves, by virtue of their innocence, in a unique position to win back something of value that was in danger of being lost? What if they willingly accepted this responsibility and paid the cost of it?

It is obvious that the suffering of which we speak is "innocent." It is not to be thought of as punishment, though it shares and bears the sorrows of a fallen world. It is not to be interpreted by a vocabulary of guilt, judgment, and condemnation arising from any wrong that has been done; for those who accept it could avoid it if they wished. It is usually inspired by love and quickened by devotion. Its vocabulary is the vocabulary of sacrifice, for it has nothing in mind but to accomplish the well-being of the beloved.

Does the suffering of the innocent have such creative power? Is it possible that it is not only *one* of the ways but *the* way in which God overcomes our guilt, fear, and estrangement? The wicked who suffer can have no complaint; but what if the innocent do not complain, but bear their suffering in such a way that it becomes an instrument of good?

THE INNOCENT FOR THE GUILTY?

This idea of the innocent choosing to suffer in the hope of accomplishing a perceived good suggests a further refinement, subtle to express but well within our experience. It is that the innocent can sometimes accomplish for the guilty what the guilty cannot accomplish for themselves. To grasp the truth of this we need only remember that this is what happens every time we forgive or are forgiven. The willingness of the innocent to take the first step towards the guilty is both the hope and means of reconciliation.

Some time ago, I talked to a woman who had been deeply wounded by the treachery of someone she loved and had trusted. Of course, none of us is ever entirely innocent in such matters, but in this instance she came pretty close. I asked her if she had made up her mind how she was going to deal with her hurt and, if she had, what it was she wished to accomplish by her decision. She replied that the estrangement meant she was separated from someone to whom she truly belonged. She wanted to restore the broken relationship if it was within her power to do so.

It Takes Two to Tango

It is one thing to state an intention, but quite another to accomplish it. How was the reconciliation she so strongly desired to be brought about? It was then that the woman spoke of the person who had wounded her, of what he must be thinking and how he must be feeling. He was a man of conscience who knew that he had behaved badly and that his conduct was unforgivable. She was afraid that his sense of shame would be so deep, and his sense of guilt so humiliating, as to preclude his having any hope that their relationship could ever be restored. His sense of unworthiness and fear of rejection might well be enough to discourage any reconciling initiative on his part.

She was not prepared to wait. She had come to see that while it is the guilty party that *ought* to take the first step in such affairs, they often cannot bring themselves to do so *because* of their guilt. They simply despair of ever being able to make up the lost ground.

It is in such circumstances that the miracle of forgiveness and reconciliation is accomplished. How does one deal with what is unpardonable? The only way to deal with it is to pardon it; the unforgivable may be forgiven; and more often than not the initiative will be taken, not by the guilty who ought to take it, but by the innocent who need not—not by the overtures of those who are in the wrong, but by the kindness of those who have been wronged. If the first gesture of reconciliation is not made by the offended, the chances are it will not be made at all. Listen to Dag Hammarskjøld on this:

> Forgiveness breaks the chain of causality because he who "forgives" you—out of love—takes upon himself the consequences of what *you* have done. Forgiveness, therefore, always entails a sacrifice.

George Macdonald does not speak of breaking a chain of causality, but takes the same insight and infuses it with emotion and wraps it in devotion:

> I prayed to God that He would make me into a rock which swallowed up the waves of wrong in its great caverns and never threw them back to swell the commotion of the angry sea whence they came. Ah, what it would be actually to annihilate wrong in this way—to be able to say, "It shall not be wrong against me, so utterly do I forgive it!"

These words are so incredibly gracious that they begin to sound too good to be true. They trigger a countersuggestion from us that they are too pure, too demanding, and too idealistic for this coarse world. They remind us of the words of C. S. Lewis that forgiveness is easy until you have to do it. But just when our skepticism moves us to the edge of cynicism and threatens to take us over, the thing happens before our eyes and authenticates itself by being done.

MARIE

My first official church appointment was to the Maguiresbridge and Lisbellaw Pastoral Charge in County Fermanagh, Northern Ireland. One of the congregations on "The Circuit," as we called it, was at Tempo where it was ably led by Tommy Watson and his wife, Margaret. Their daughter Joan was the organist there, though she lived in Belfast where she was training to be a teacher.

Joan was later to marry Gordon Wilson of Enniskillen, whom I also knew. Gordon's sister is the wife of Dr. Hedley Plunkett, the minister largely responsible for my entering the Christian ministry. Gordon and Joan Wilson had two children, Peter and Marie. Marie became a nurse and worked in the Royal Victoria Hospital, Belfast.

On a weekend in November she returned to Enniskillen to visit her parents and went with her father to the War Memorial in the town to honor those who had died in the two World Wars. It was then that a bomb planted by the I.R.A. went off, burying Gordon and Marie under a heap of rubble.

Gordon's account of the hours they spent together while waiting to be rescued is heart-wrenching. Marie comforted her father and kept reassuring him. Four or five times he called to her, "Are you all right?" and each time she replied, "Yes! I'm fine!" but her answers became less confident. She gripped her father's hand tightly under the debris and called out to him, "Daddy, I love you very much." Those were the last words he ever heard her speak. She was twenty years old.

When Gordon was interviewed by Mike Gaston, a BBC reporter, he told him that he had lost his daughter but bore no grudge or ill will. Bitter talk would not bring her back. He did not mention forgiveness in the broadcast, but people understood it was forgiveness he was talking about. He later wrote, "I'm not going to add to the hatreds by talking about revenge. I'll go on praying for all of them." Gordon and Joan Wilson prayed for Marie's murderers every day. Gordon is dead now. And so is Peter, who was killed in an accident. And Joan continues her work as organist of Darling Street Methodist Church, Enniskillen.

As I write this, it has been announced that David Trimble and John Hume have been awarded the Nobel Peace Prize for their efforts to bring peace to Ireland. But David Trimble and John Hume would be the first to acknowledge that what they accomplished would not have been possible but for men and women like Gordon and Joan Wilson who "broke the chain of causality" and took upon themselves the consequences of the actions of wicked men. They did it by swallowing up the waves of wrong, and never throwing them back to swell the commotion of the angry sea of hate whence they came. They actually annihilated wrong by saying "It shall not be wrong against me, so utterly do I forgive it!"

FINDING THE RIGHT HANDLE

Epictetus the Stoic helps to make this plain in another way when he tells us that everything has two handles; by one we can carry it, and by the other we can't. He gives us an example: Suppose our brother has offended us. If we wish, we may attempt to carry the estrangement by the handle of the offense; but if we do, the alienation will be made more bitter by our brooding on it.

On the other hand, we may decide to carry the estrangement, not by the handle of the offense, but by the handle of the relationship. We may say to ourselves, "There is no doubt that he

has offended me; but he is my brother!" In this way lies the best
hope of reconciliation; and it is usually the work of the injured
party to initiate it.

When the innocent enable the guilty to do what the guilty
cannot do for themselves, we may catch a glimpse of the
"Suffering Servant" of whom Isaiah speaks in four of the greatest chapters of his book. The Suffering Servant is the One whom
God has chosen to effect the consolation of Israel, to heal the
wounds and forgive the sins of His people by taking upon himself the cost of their reconciliation.

It would be hard to exaggerate how deeply Isaiah's thought
has affected the way we think of suffering, or how profoundly he
has influenced our interpretation of life and faith. The prophet's
avowal that suffering may be vicarious, that it may be willingly undertaken on behalf of others, and for their sake, was taken
up by Jesus of Nazareth, who understood His own life and death
in the light of it.

TURNING FAITH ON ITS HEAD

A serious misunderstanding that distorts Christian faith and
turns people from it is their confusion concerning the *direction* of
the work of Christ. This produces a host of what George
Macdonald called "mean theologies" and asks us to believe that
God behaves in ways that are not worthy of Him.

Our mistake is to think that everything Jesus sought to
accomplish was directed towards God in an attempt to placate
His wrath, or to argue Him into kindness, or to convince Him
that we are not as bad as He thinks we are. Jesus is for us, but God
is against us. God is so righteous and just, and so easily offended,
that we cannot enjoy His approval. He must be won from hostility to mercy, and it is the work of Jesus to accomplish it.

To believe this is to set Christian faith on its head. It is to
distort the most essential truth of it, namely that the work of

Jesus is God's work. The purpose of Jesus was not to persuade God to be gracious, but to show us how gracious God is; not to overcome God's enmity, but to save us from our guilt, fear, and distrust; not to win God over, but to persuade us that if we ever thought He was against us, we were mistaken.

What Jesus did, both by the quality of His life and the manner of His death, is God's way of showing us how much He loves us. By His coming into the world Jesus declared that God loves us enough to share our humanity and become incarnate for our sake. His task was not to reconcile God to us, but to bring us back to God. God did not need the cross of Christ in order to forgive us—He had forgiven multitudes before Christ ever was born—we needed it in order to understand what God's forgiveness means, and to be won to repentance and faith.

Lost!

We are often told that the meaning of God's reconciling love is that if we will repent, and will return to Him, He will receive and forgive us. Now, that is true. The only trouble with it is that it begs the question; and the question is, How are we to repent? We suppose that our repentance is our work, and that forgiving us is God's work; but it is not quite as simple as that; and the truth is more gracious than that. Our penitence, too, is God's work. It is God's loving initiative that brings us to repentance. The truth is not that we repent and then God forgives us; it is that God's forgiveness of us is His bringing us to repentance. We are not forgiven because we repent, we repent because we are forgiven. John Donne put it perfectly:

> Here on this lowly ground,
> Teach me how to repent;

> For that's as good
> As if Thou hadst sealed my pardon
> With Thy blood.

When our daughter Jennifer was a tiny girl, we lost her at Brigden Fair. Brigden is a small Ontario town, famous for its Fall Fair, which attracts great crowds from all over the county. But at Brigden Fair we blinked our eyes, and Jennifer was gone. Sick with fright, we searched for her. We discovered that "the taste of fear" is a literal truth and that the throat can so ache from anxiety that it is hard to swallow. Imagination went wild. We thought of that precious little fragment of humanity, lost, bewildered, and terrified among the animals and all the people and the confusion of stalls, booths, and roundabouts.

Fifteen minutes later, we found her. She had been wandering nonchalantly about the place, having the time of her life. She was just beginning to be the center of interest and was enjoying every minute of it. I can still feel the sense of relief and overwhelming joy at seeing her dear face and taking her small hand. But the truth is that Jennifer did not know she was lost until we found her.

We may think that the meaning of God's reconciling love is that when the lost return, the lost are welcomed and forgiven. But it is better than that: it is that God has come to us in Christ "to seek and to save that which was lost."

Two poems tell the difference. One of them assures us that even if Little Bo Peep should lose her sheep and not know where to find them, all she need do is leave them alone. If she does, then they will return home, "wagging their tails behind them." The other poem has something deeper and darker to tell us:

> But none of the ransomed ever knew
> How deep were the waters crossed;
> Nor how dark was the night that the Lord
> passed through
> Ere He found His sheep that was lost.

P. T. Forsythe, a distinguished theologian and teacher of preachers, used to say to his students, "Don't tell people how they ought to feel about Christ. Preach a Christ who will make them feel how they ought to feel."

"YOU'LL NEVER KNOW IF YOU DON'T KNOW NOW"

This is the kind of truth that can be told only by being done. Some truths are like that. How am I to convince you that I love you enough to marry you, except by marrying you? Saying it is not enough; I can tell it only by doing it. Miss Eliza Doolittle is tired of words: "Show me!" she demands. And that is what God did when His Word was made flesh and came to dwell among us, full of grace and truth. His Word not only tells us by being spoken, but shows us by being done. As the Scriptures say, "By this we have come to believe the love God has for us."

Seventy years ago, D. S. Cairns expressed this eloquently:

It is quite clear that the whole teaching of Jesus Christ about God, expressed alike in His words and in the whole fashion and mold of His character, implies that God is always nearer, mightier, more loving, and more free to help every one of us than any one of us ever realizes. This alone is what makes His incessant summons to faith, and to more faith, coherent and reasonable. This again seems to me to imply that mankind is generally under a hypnotic spell about God, which is always contracting and chilling their thoughts of Him and leading to all kinds of depressing and terrifying illusions about Him.

All God's dealings with us are for us, and not for Him; everything He seeks to accomplish is in our interest, not His. From first motive to latest intent there is nothing in God but goodness acting on our behalf. Even when He resists us, it is for our sake. He wants nothing for Himself and desires nothing but the best for us. He loves us, not for His profit, but for ours.

ON BEING ALL-OF-A-PIECE

However much we might wish it, such magnanimity is beyond us. Knowing our own heart, we know the limits of our altruism and are aware that even when our love is at its deepest, fiercest, and most passionate, it is infused with self-interest.

Ogden Nash has a poem in which he tells of a man called Orlando Tregennis, who loved his wife so much that he decided to climb a high mountain and name it after her. And that is what he did, and called the mountain, "Mount Mrs. Orlando Tregennis." Yeats told Anne Gregory that he had heard an old religious man declare that only God "could love you for yourself alone, and not your yellow hair." The poet is right: God does not love Anne Gregory for her yellow hair. He loves her, as He loves all His children, for herself alone.

It is this perfection of love, perfectly revealed in His Son, that constitutes the innocence of Jesus. Such purity of heart is neither naive nor passive, but discerning, integrative, and active. It means that He was all-of-a-piece, so that the impulse of His heart, the thought of His mind, the word of His mouth, and the action of His hand were one single flame.

We aspire to, but never achieve, such wholeness. We suffer from what William James called "our torn-to-piecesness." We are incapable of revealing anything perfectly, for we are a bundle of contradictions in ourselves. But in Jesus there was no division, no commingled motives, no confused intent. He spoke and acted unanimously. With total transparency the true Son truly revealed His Father's heart.

"THE HAIRSBREADTH BETWEEN
BLACK AND WHITE"

We know how the world He loved treated Him:

> He was in the world; but the world, though
> it owed its being to him, did not recognize him.
> He entered his own realm, and his own would
> not receive him. (NEB)

To say that His own would not receive Him is to speak of His crucifixion.

It is easy to imagine the ghosts of Virgil, Job, Daniel, and the psalmist gathering round that event—and with them the spirits of all who ever pondered the plight of the innocent, or lamented the injustice of the world, or tried to make sense of human ills and the divine ordering of things. By showing us what evil did to blameless love, the crucifixion of Christ draws into itself not only our persistent questions but also our hesitant answers, and focuses them to a point of sharpest intensity.

"THE COMMUNION OF SAINTS"

Here the drama of all innocent suffering, and what can be made of it, and what may be accomplished by means of it, is played out for us. In this one happening we see the things that "have their tears," and listen to Job's lament at the absence of God; here the psalmist's complaint that the righteous receive no special favors is definitively depicted, and Isaiah's Suffering Servant is placarded before our eyes. Here, too, Daniel's hope that in dying we die into God, and therefore into life, meets its decisive test and receives its ultimate vindication.

Never were the issues more precisely delineated, and never was the choice between faith and cynicism more unequivocally presented. Here, in one happening, both the temptation to "curse God and die," and the invitation to affirm "though He slay me, yet will I trust Him," are lucidly displayed and plainly offered.

Our artists have always known this intuitively. They perceive that in all the varied interpretations of the crucifixion they attempt to portray, there is something so starkly wicked, and so sublimely noble, that in this one event, and in one and the same moment, we may be seduced by despair or captured by faith.

That is what it meant to Graham Sutherland, who in 1946 painted "Crucifixion." The picture hangs in The Tate Gallery, London, and on a plaque which rests beside the painting are the words of the artist:

> It is the most tragic of all themes, yet inherent in it is the promise of salvation. It is the symbol of the precarious balanced moment, the hairsbreadth between black and white.

The symbol that threatens to overwhelm us by the evil it exposes is the symbol that invites our allegiance by the love it reveals.

In the cross of Christ, time and eternity meet, for universal experience is clumped in the immediacy of history, and ultimate truth is expressed in a fugitive moment. Here we learn from one solitary life that life is tragic, that the blameless suffer, and that love must pay a frightful price to accomplish its purposes.

VICTIM OR VICTOR?

We have noticed that around the cross of Christ were gathered, not only the women who loved Him and the soldiers who crucified Him, but the shades of all who ever lamented the suffering of the innocent or asked why, if God is good, the world should be the way it is.

Yet it would be a grave error to suppose that the usefulness of the cross of Christ is merely to serve as a repository of righteous complaint, or an exposé of the baseness of evil, or a focus of the world's injustice. As we have seen, it does all of these things uniquely; yet it is, first and foremost, the decisive act in which God not only reveals the horror of wickedness, but engages and defeats it. The crucifixion is not a summing up, but a saving action. It is not primarily about what the world did to Jesus, but about what God has done for the world. It not only unmasks the vileness of evil but announces that God has overcome evil with good. It not only reveals what wickedness people may do when estranged from God; it is the means by which God reconciles them to Himself.

The definitive action in the crucifixion is, therefore, not man's, but God's. Everything that was brought against Jesus, He straightened to His own purpose and shaped to His own design. At the end of it He could declare His work "finished." As Moses accomplished the Exodus from Egypt, so Christ, the second Moses, accomplished His Exodus in Jerusalem by leading God's people from captivity to freedom, from the land of bondage to "the country of the Great King."

CHRISTUS VICTOR

That is why the day on which He was crucified is "Good" Friday, that is, God's Friday. It does not belong to His executioners, but to the Victim who reigns from the tree. On that day, human hatred was transformed into a divine opportunity for good, suffering became the instrument of grace, a sense of God forsakenness was the occasion of deeper trust, and death the opportunity to sink but deeper into God. The day on which evil did its worst is the day on which hatred, suffering, and death were overwhelmed, swallowed up in the triumph of love, faith, and life.

We crucified Christ. What He crucified was every mean theology, every idea of God we have ever had that is not worthy of us or of Him. God is not our enemy, but our Friend. He is not against us, but with us, and for us, and in us. If we ever doubted it, we can do so no longer; for "God has proved His love for us by laying down His life for our sake." The truth of this was perfectly expressed in another time and at another place by Joseph in Egypt at the beginning of Israel's history when he told his brothers who had done him great hurt, "You meant it unto me for evil, but God meant it for good."

The news of Christ's triumph broke upon the world on Easter morning when the sun rose on an empty tomb; but the victory was won before sunset on Good Friday:

> Before the westering sun went down, . . .
> He knew that He had won.

This was our Lord's way of ratifying His exhortation and assurance to His disciples as He moved to accomplish His death:

> In the world you will have trouble. But courage!
> The victory is mine; I have conquered the world. (NEB)

The cross of Christ is still God's action on our behalf. The forgiveness of God is not a grudging word of reluctant pardon spoken to us when we decide to return to Him; it is everything He ever did, and all that He continues to do, to awaken our faith and accomplish our repentance. God's forgiveness of us is much more than His response to our remorse; it is His kindling of our love by the tenderness of His own when He loved us to death with every drop of His life. It is not anything we need to win by any initiative of our own, but a gift we receive by the mercy and travail of God. Here is how Bunyan's Pilgrim experienced it:

Then was Christian glad and lightsome, and said with a merry heart, "He hath given me rest by His sorrow, and life by his death." Then he stood still a while to look and wonder, for it was very surprising to him that the sight of the cross should thus ease him of his burden. . . . Then Christian gave three leaps for joy, and went out singing. . . .

CHAPTER SEVENTEEN

CHIPMUNKS
AND
CHILDREN

I think of this work of reconciliation every time I go to my summer cottage and attempt to make friends with the chipmunks and squirrels who live there. It is an annual event, for the summer friendships do not survive the winter's separation.

When I arrive, the little creatures keep what they must think is a healthy distance from me, behaving as though I were an intruder trespassing on their property and regarding me with the utmost suspicion and resentment. The squirrels are more boisterous than their cousins. They find a safe branch and, quivering with righteous indignation, complain and scold me for violating their space. Most of the time it is a solitary scold, but they sometimes organize themselves into hostile duets, trios, or quartets of cacophonous outrage.

As the days pass, relationships improve. We grow easier with each other because I address them respectfully in their own language and punctuate our conversations with a roasted peanut here and a roasted peanut there. The chipmunks are the first to surrender their suspicion and turn friendly. This is a great help in winning over the squirrels, for they cannot bear to see their small relatives scurrying off to their holes-in-the-ground with cheeks stuffed and stretched almost to bursting with booty.

By the second week of July we arrive at the degree of intimacy achieved by the second week of July a year earlier. By this time I have convinced them that I mean them no harm; that they do not need to be afraid; that if they come to visit and wish to sit on my hand, they will be safe and I shall be pleased.

On Not Crossing Jordan

Little did I realize that overcoming the hostility and winning the trust of small rodents would serve me well as a preparation for dealing with small children. I was to discover it not long after the birth of my granddaughter, Jordan. I was out of the country when Jordan was born, so that by the time of our first encounter she was old enough to regard me with a wary eye. Her mother was holding her at the time of our introduction, and Jordan chose to stay in her mother's arms as though fixed there by a strip of Velcro. She would have nothing at all to do with me. When I spoke, she did not answer. When I smiled, she frowned. When I tried to catch her eye, she turned her face away in the manner of a New York waiter and resisted all efforts to engage her. What was her grandfather to do?

What he did was make the confrontation into a game. When she turned her head away from me, I turned to meet her. When she turned back, then I did, too. By the time we had done this twenty times, I was a little dizzy and she had begun to enjoy herself. Next, I touched her perfect ankle, and then her dimpled knee; then her wrist, and fingers, and hair and cheek; and while this was going on, I whispered to her in her own language. At last, she responded with the faintest of smiles. Then she pointed. Then she said something. Then she showed me her hand. And then she reached out her arms to be gathered into mine.

"You Made Me Love You"

We sometimes complain that it is hard to understand what the Scriptures mean when they tell us that "God was in Christ reconciling the world unto Himself." Yet we ourselves have accomplished a reconciling work on many an occasion and in a manner that is perfectly understandable. What we need to realize is that God does it as we do it, though He thought of it first, and does it better, and at greater cost, and with far more people, and with far more difficult people than we are likely to meet. For while we may attempt to reconcile our estranged friends and loved ones, God seeks to reconcile the world.

In His Son, God overcomes our suspicion, awakens our trust, kindles our love, smiles us into smiling, and loves us into loving in the same way that I accomplished these things for my little granddaughter. In Jesus of Nazareth, God came seeking us and showed us His love and told us that we don't need to be afraid. Jesus is God's way of touching our ankle, and our elbow, and our knee, and our cheek, until we so trust and love Him that we stretch out our arms to be taken into His. This is what we mean when we say that by the work of Christ God reconciles us to Himself.

What we have just written may seem too simple and sentimental to be of any real use in helping us to understand the ways of God or the work of Christ. Yet a thing can be simple, and rich with sentiment, and still be true. It is Jesus Himself who tells us that we should call God *Abba,* which not only sounds like our "dada" or "mamma" but is, like them, among the first names children learn to call their father and mother. It surely follows that if Jesus encourages us to think of God in such a personal, individual, and intimate way it is because God thinks of us in the same way. He cherishes us as His dear children, the offspring of His heart, the little ones of His love's conceiving. According to Jesus, our best clue to understanding God's way with us is found in our way with our children.

A CLUE TO THE BARD

Wiser heads than ours, indeed, have told us that homey hints may illumine profound matters, and tentative intimations may truly characterize the reality they can only hint at. If we attempt to understand the inspiration of Scripture or of Shakespeare, for example, our best help may be found, not in the mystery of Shakespeare's mind, but in the more familiar workings of our own. There are times when singers no longer carry a tune but are carried on wings of song; dancers may discover that their limbs can accomplish without effort what they had striven to achieve; the actor's lines may sometimes come to meet him, already possessed; writers occasionally write better than they can write; and composers may find the air "full of sounds and sweet airs that give delight and hurt not." This does not mean that we have it in us to write Lear or Hamlet; it does mean that in those spirited moments when our own house is haunted, we spy something of what it means to be inspired.

WHAT IS IT WE HAVE DONE?

What are we to learn from this sweeping view that has taken us from Joseph, the Hebrew prince of Egypt, to Dag Hammarskjøld, a Secretary General of the United Nations? We may learn, as we have already stated, that we are not alone in our distress at the ills that have afflicted, and continue to torment, so many; nor are we the first to complain about the injustice of the world or to try and make sense of its puzzlement.

Beyond that, we may benefit from the insight and experience of the great ones we have mentioned, for they have helpful things to say to us. They have long pondered the questions that proved so troubling to them and are so perplexing to us. Now they have wisdom to share with us, truth that is theirs only by the experience of discovering it, living it, and making it their own, often at great cost.

We must not speak of innocent suffering as though we never heard of Job or as if we did not know that when the divine life came among us, it was crucified. We should not expect prosperity to be the reward of virtue or assume that the good life is invariably a success story, attained by positive thinking and authenticated by health, wealth, and length of days.

Listening to Isaiah or Daniel, we shall never again believe that our pain is proof of our guilt or assume that if we are afflicted it is because we are wicked. We cannot now regard our troubles as a divine punishment or conclude that God is against us in our distress, or that He approves of it. We shall not find ourselves wondering why God sent it to us, or what we did to deserve it, but recognize His presence in the strength by which we bear it. We shall affirm that if God is present in our troubles, it is not as the enemy who sends them, but as the Friend who bears them. We shall not blame Him for our hurts, but discover Him in our healing.

Yet there is more. We should have learned from these dissidents and pioneers of faith that suffering is not anything we need to gather into belief, for the faith into which we seek to gather it already contains it. Nor is it merely "factored in" as we might say of some new data that might affect the stock market. Evil and suffering are not external to faith, waiting to be factored either in or out, but lie at the heart of it, are inseparable from it, and define its nature. We cannot introduce the suffering of the innocent into faith, for the faith into which we think to bring it already contains it, and is defined by its awareness of it and the use it makes of it.

When as a young man I was faced with the sadness of a young woman's death, and decided I had to either gather it into faith or lose faith itself, my attitude was conceited and foolish. We do not need to gather the pain of this world into faith; what we need is to rightly understand the faith that not only carries as its symbol "the wondrous cross, where the young Prince of Glory died," but offers us a share in "the fellowship of His sufferings."

CHAPTER EIGHTEEN

"DELIVER US FROM EVIL"

THE MAN BORN BLIND

*T*he disciples of Jesus one day saw a man who had been blind from birth and were prompted to ask whose sin had caused his affliction: "Rabbi, who sinned, this man or his parents? Why was he born blind?"

They attempted to understand the blindness by connecting it with sin, guilt, and punishment in a direct causal relation. It was in a vocabulary of such words that the suffering was to be described and interpreted. It was not a question of *whether* there was a causal relation between sin and suffering; the disciples simply assumed that there was, so that the only question was *whose* sin had caused it, the man's own or that of his parents.

It is a nice question, and we might suppose that the disciples thought they were in for a lengthy discussion of morals, religion, and philosophy. What they got was nothing of the sort. Jesus simply described the man's affliction, but in a different vocabulary, and healed him.

RELATIVES AND CAUSAL RELATIONS

In a single sentence, Jesus denied the direct, immediate, and causal relation between sin and suffering when He said, "It is not that this man or his parents sinned." He had already stated this position when He had been asked about the Galileans whom Pilate had slaughtered and the others who had perished when the Tower of Siloam fell on them. On that occasion He had answered the question of their guilt and punishment by saying that the people who had been killed were not any more wicked than those who escaped.

This blind man, then, was not afflicted with blindness because someone had sinned. His suffering was not to be understood as a punishment for wickedness. His blindness was not an invitation to condemn either him or his parents, for the three of them had suffered enough; it was, in the present circumstances, an opportunity to give the man his sight. Jesus then showed the disciples what He meant by opening the man's eyes so that he could see.

When the disciples considered the blind man's predicament, they thought the divine action was located in God's punishment of some sin, real or imagined. Jesus said that God's action was to be discerned, not in the affliction, but in the healing of it. The only "meaning" in the blindness was that it might become an occasion of grace.

We have all wondered, at some time or other, what we would do if great suffering came to us or if we were informed that our life would soon be over. How would we bear it? How do we like to think we should bear it?

AGAINST US FOR OUR SAKE

The first thing, surely, is to refuse to think badly of God, who is not the One who leads us into temptation, but the One who delivers us from evil. Our afflictions, then, are no reason to curse God, as Job's wife suggested her husband should do, but to trust Him, as Job did. If we wish to discover where God is to be found in our distress, then we should believe our Lord when He tells us that He is to be found in the bearing of it, not in the sending of it. He comes, not to afflict, but as the Bearer of grace, forgiveness, strength, and healing.

We must never think that our suffering means that God is against us. God is never against us, except for our sake, which means that He is always for us. When we are afflicted, those who strive to make us well are not working against God; they are the instruments of His goodness, whether or not they are aware of it. We must not take our suffering to mean that we are inordinately sinful folk being singled out for affliction, in an unusual way, to punish our extraordinary wickedness.

We should recognize, of course, that pain and suffering are sometimes the result of particular habits and kinds of behavior for which we are obviously and directly responsible. If we smoke heavily, for example, or eat unwisely, or drink excessively, or are sexually irresponsible, or engage in hazardous occupations or hobbies, we should not be surprised if our conduct sometimes has an unhealthy outcome. And if it has, we should not feel that it is something for which God is to blame or that we have been personally chosen for special affliction. We should admit that the outcome of our conduct was largely predictable and that we might well have avoided it if we had chosen to do so.

We should recognize, too, that the same sort of causal relation pertains, not only to physical interaction, but to personal relationships as well. If we are untrustworthy or disloyal to our friends, for example, we will not expect them to respond with warm affection and genial trust. Yet causal relations of this sort are for our benefit, for we can learn to understand them and allow our knowledge to direct and modify our behavior.

We ought also to remember that, as we have said, troubles come and are not sent; and accidents happen but are not caused. This means that troubles may come to anyone and that an accident is no respecter of persons.

We shall not be surprised, then, if in the normal course of events troubles come and accidents happen to us or to those whom we love. When they do, we shall not suffer the sometimes overwhelming mental anguish of wondering what we did to deserve them, or try to discover some connection between our suffering and our sin, or rail against God for sending them. We shall regard them as our part of the anguish of a suffering world, and learn to deal with them as well as we can. But how well is that?

ALL THINGS WORKING OR GOD COOPERATING?

An oft-quoted text from the King James Version of the Scriptures assures us that "all things work together for good to them that love God." The text, alas, is not only a poor translation, but what it says is not true. All things frequently do not work together for good, even for those who love God. The *New English Bible* gives us both a better translation and a more helpful insight when it tells us that "in everything, as we know, [God] cooperates for good with those who love God."

This means that God is already present and at work in all the evils that afflict us, seeking to bring good out of them. It does not deny that they are evils; it does not sentimentalize them or pretend that they are really goods in disguise. It does mean that God's work is to bring good out of evil by His own wisdom and love and with the help of those with whom He cooperates for good. Think of what it would mean to collaborate with God in this way!

One of the ways in which God cooperates for good is by enabling us to so bear our afflictions that they are not permitted to become the occasion of greater ills. They might easily become that if we allowed them to produce in us a bitter harvest of self-pity, unbelief, and despair. These attitudes would be new evils, to be added to the evil that produced them. And their effect would be apparent, not only in the bleakness of the wounded spirit, but in the contagion it would spread to other spirits.

If, on the other hand, we find grace to bear our troubles with courage, cheerfulness, and a quiet mind, then we have not only kept evil from producing more evil; we have overcome evil with good. Once again, the effect will be apparent not only in the faith and hope and love of those who suffer, but in the power of their example. Others gain their courage from those of a noble spirit. That is why we must never stop believing that it matters how we bear ourselves. Hammarskjøld was right: we should die with decency so that at least decency will survive. To do so is not merely the hope of victory; it is itself the victory.

As Though They Had Been Sent

Everything we have said has insisted that troubles are not sent; they come. We are not singled out by God for specific ills directed at us in particular. Yet many of those who have dealt most profitably with the troubles that have come to them have done so by treating them *as though* they had been sent.

They have not believed that they were. They have not thought that God singled them out in any unloving way. Indeed, it is because they are so sure of His love for them, and so certain that He is with them in their affliction, that they have come to think of it as something shared with Him. Their troubles have not succeeded in estranging them from God or in setting them over against Him in complaint and grievance, but have drawn them to Him in a new realization of how much their faith and love matter in His overcoming of evil. It is this conviction that refreshes their courage and heartens their resolve.

It is as though God had initiated them into some secret that so deepened their sense of divine companionship that they came to believe they were bearing their suffering, not only with Him, but for Him. They have not only considered the sufferings of Christ, but have discovered that their own pain has given them such kinship with Him that they have been brought to share in what the Scriptures call "the fellowship of His suffering." In short, they have come to regard the troubles that have randomly come to them as a trust from God.

"AMONG THE FARTHEST HEBRIDES"

This spirit of trust is poignantly unveiled for us in the true story of the young couple and their only child who dwelt in a lone cottage on one of the Hebridean islands. Their little one became so gravely ill that in spite of all their efforts there was no betterment for her. After a long day of anxious vigil, when it was clear that she would not last the night, the father said to the mother, "It seems that God is going to take our little girl." And the mother replied with all the nobility, grace, and faith of the island people, "We must not allow God to take our little one; we must give her to Him." And so they knelt together and placed the child of their heart in the strong and tender hands that had formed both her and them.

One could scarcely write such things were it not for our knowledge of those who have accomplished them. Once again, the temptation is so to describe the valiant bearing of suffering as to gloss over the appalling nature of it and underestimate the horror of it. We may think such grace as we have described almost unbelievable, and far beyond anything we could ever achieve; yet we cannot pretend that others have not attained it, and we may venture the hope that we might gain our courage from their example. When Leslie Weatherhead visited his sister for the last time, her words to him as he left her darkened room were, "Go on preaching, Leslie; what you preach is true. I am proud to be trusted with cancer. I pray that I may not miss the message that is hidden in every pain."

Once again, this does not mean that God sends us pain in order to send us a message or to teach us a lesson. He doesn't "send" it at all. It does mean that when suffering comes we may ask what we might gain from it. The suffering is there anyway, and the brutal fact of it cannot be avoided; why, it is as though it occupied space. We must decide what we are going to do with it, for we must do *something* with it. We may deal with it well or badly; and one of the most helpful ways of dealing with it is to try and learn something from it, and in this way bring good out of it. Reinhold Niebuhr, for example, thought it a useful thing to ask, "What ultimate use, what final point for the grace of God is there in this calamity?"

THE ENCHANTED LOOM

One of the virtues of his framing of the question is that it both retains the sense of calamity and affirms the action of grace. It reminds us that joy and sorrow do not exclude each other, that the choice is not joy *or* sorrow because, as Paul tells us, "in our sorrows we have always cause for joy." Joy and sorrow are inseparable because each finds its depth and fullness by gathering the other's nature into its own. It is neither the candle, nor the wick, but the burning; it is neither the joy nor the sorrow, but the weaving:

> Joy and woe are woven fine,
> A clothing for the soul divine.
> Under every grief and pine
> Runs a joy with silken twine.
> It is right it should be so;
> Man was made for joy and woe.
> And when this we rightly know,
> Through the world we safely go.

Indeed, in those lines we find a way to understand, not only the weaving of our joy and sorrow, but the braiding of our life and death. That is how Paul understood our disintegration and renewal, our dying and our being raised to life. He explicitly says so:

No wonder we do not lose heart! Though our outward humanity is in decay, yet day by day we are inwardly renewed. Our troubles are slight and short-lived; and their outcome an eternal glory which outweighs them far. (NEB)

This is God's deliverance of us from evil; it is deliverance from the decline of life and the contradiction of death.

The Ending Worthy of the Drama?

Malcolm Muggeridge used to say that he believed in eternal life because he believed that the ending would be worthy of the drama. In this he echoes Saint Paul who speaks of a coming glory that outweighs all our troubles. But Paul also tells us that we may daily live the daily drama in such a way as to not only anticipate its ending but participate in its "end," that is, its meaning and purpose, the reason why there is a drama in the first place.

We can do it, says Paul, by refusing to think that death is merely something that happens to us at the end of our life. That is how we think of it: first we live, and then we die; we then try to put off thinking about it for as long as we can.

Paul will have none of it. Death is not something that follows life in succession, it is something that we accomplish in life. Life and death are going on at the same time. Every moment of our living is a moment of our dying. It might all be expressed in a sentence: We live into death and die into life; and we do so, not consecutively, but simultaneously. Our living and our dying, like our joy and our sorrow, are not two things, but one. George Macdonald puts it perfectly: "We die daily. Happy are those who daily come to life as well."

There is an obvious sense of this that is beyond contradiction. We daily live into death by the decline and final disintegration of what Paul calls "our outward humanity," the "dear ruin" that we all finally become notwithstanding our creams, diets, vitamins, potions, injections, medicines, treatments, exercising, tinting, manicuring, reshaping, replacing, remaking, transplanting.

DYING INTO LIFE

And yet, while daily living into death we are dying into life. We die into life when we die to ourselves and come alive for others. As George Macdonald put it, "You will be dead so long as you refuse to die." We have glimpses of this in so simple a thing as a conversation in which we truly "lend our minds out" and make another person the soul of our awareness. We die into life by loving our children more than ourselves. Lovers die into life all the time, for what is life in oneself compared with life in the beloved? Philip Larkin knew about that. He tells us it is a matter of "Counting," reminding us that although thinking in terms of one is easily done, counting up to two is harder: "For one must be denied, before it's tried."

Those who die into life measure their age, not by the weakness of their body, but by the strength of their spirit. By the time they come to the end of their life, much of their dying has been already done. There is little that can be taken from them, for they have already given it away. Death is not merely something that happens to a Christian; it is something a Christian may accomplish. In a lovely phrase Emily Dickinson speaks of "the overtakelessness of those who have *accomplished* death."

LOVE'S LABOR LOST?

Yet it seems that we are overtaken by death, for we all die. Death is the denial, the contradiction of everything, the final "No!" to the "Yes!" of creation. It mocks our search for meaning and wrecks our belief in any loving purpose for the world. It denies the goodness and power of God by making it clear that if He ever intended to accomplish anything in us, or make something of us, it must come to nothing, for He will not have time to finish it.

In short, death makes any coherent theodicy impossible, for who could hope to "justify the ways of God to men" if the divine purpose must be accomplished in so short a time as our temporal life allows? Paul is exactly right:

> If it is for this life only that Christ has given us hope, we of all men are most to be pitied. (NEB)

Paul, of course, does not believe it for a moment, because this death, too, is a dying into life. He knows it, as we do, from the faith of Israel and the character of God, from the deeds and promises of Christ, and from His resurrection. He knows it from the testimony of the Apostles and other witnesses and from his own sight of his risen Lord. And he knows it as one who has friendship with an immortal Christ and is held by a Love that already reaches him from beyond the grave.

Paul is so sure that the good purposes of God will not be frustrated that he writes his certainty to his friends at Philippi by telling them that "the One who started the good work in you will bring it to completion" (NEB). And he exhorts his friends at Corinth to work without ceasing in the assurance that "their labors are not in vain and cannot be lost." My goodness, in places he even anticipates his own reward!

THE HELL OF IT

No theodicy can survive the traditional belief in hell by which an innumerable multitude of souls are kept alive in eternal torment. It is suffering without end or outcome. The magnitude of such horror is unimaginable, like trying to think of all the stars in the universe. As near as I can come to imagining it is to recall the most appalling pictures of the holocaust and multiply them a billion times. But then, I cannot imagine even the horror of the holocaust, let alone something a billion times worse.

If we could imagine it, how could we keep our sanity? Surely it is only from lack of imagination that we can believe in everlasting punishment at all. To see one soul tortured is more than most of us could bear, and we should damn the torturer, not adore and worship him.

When I was a child, I was taught what the scriptures teach: that God is the One who knows, judges, and reveals the secrets of our hearts. This knowledge would be openly declared and God's verdict announced on the Day of Judgment. As it was assumed that all secrets, even those of childish hearts, were guilty secrets, Judgment Day became the stuff of nightmares— a terrifying day of shocking revelations, acute embarrassment, fierce condemnation, and overwhelming horror. How the spirit shrank at the thought of it!

Now this frightful prospect need not be read into the words of scripture themselves, yet there were always those who would load them up with enough nasty ideas to ensure that God's knowledge and telling of our secrets was a prospect to be dreaded. To this day I remember a chorus they used to sing:

> Oh, how sad it will be,
> On that Great Judgment morning,
> To be cast out of heaven
> For not loving God!

"A DAMNABLE DOCTRINE"

All that God knew of us came from information that had been taken down to be used as evidence against us. It consisted, for the most part, of knowing how bad we were. It was written indelibly in a great book that would be opened and read aloud on the last day of the world to titillate every trivial mind, indulge every incorrigible gossip, and embarrass anyone with an ounce of sensitivity.

A guilty verdict being inevitable, it was followed at once by a sentence of eternal punishment—everlasting separation from God by God's own decree. It seemed immoderate to punish temporal sins with eternal torment; this was surely a most indelicate balance, for it was hard to imagine any wickedness heinous enough to warrant such prolonged misery. And besides, there was no point to it, for it would bring no joy to the blessed and could offer no help to the damned.

Little wonder, then, that some declared the arrangement immoral and turned from faith because of it. Charles Darwin was one of them. It was not Darwin's science that drove him from faith, but the sort of "mean theology" we are describing. Darwin refused to believe what he called the "damnable doctrine" that those whom he most loved and honored would be condemned and consigned to everlasting suffering. Only the righteous seemed satisfied with this ordering of things. Who were the righteous? Why, those who knew they were, and told us so.

The thing to notice is that the judgment of God need not be understood in the terrible way we have described. Indeed, even as a child I sensed that there was something wrong with the things I was being told and that the goodness of God couldn't be as bad as it sounded. I knew, without knowing that I knew, that even God must suffer at the hands of His interpreters, that small men would make God small, and that cruel men would fashion Him after their own image. I have discovered since then how much truth there may be in a child's intuition.

THE TODDLER AND THE TYPEWRITER

What if God's perfect knowledge is not a reason for Him to condemn us, but the measure of His intimacy with us? The scriptures tell us that God knows us at the depth of our groaning. If He does, then it must mean that He knows us better than we know ourselves, for our groans are, of their very nature, inarticulate. They are wrung from us when we do not understand and cannot express the depth of what we feel, when the mystery of our own heart bewilders us.

But if God knows our hearts better than we do, it means that He can read between our lines, understand our silences, and take the meaning that is often hidden behind, under, or over our words. In this way He satisfies our need to be acknowledged, understood, and accepted.

When my daughter Jennifer was a very small girl she managed to get to my typewriter one evening and struck the keys at random and with all the abandon of a three-year-old. She then presented me with the piece of paper she had covered with scattered letters in any old order and asked me what it said. And I told her.

May we not say that God, who knows us better than we know ourselves, and reads us truly, tells our secrets, not to embarrass us to others, but to interpret us to ourselves? The secrets of God's revealing are not so much ours as His—what He has always known about us and now shows to us, as we are able to bear it. It is not that we have discovered these things and entrusted them to Him, but that He has always known them, and discloses them to us. In this way this Teller of Secrets gives us to ourselves.

RUNNING TO JUDGMENT

We may well shrink from such knowledge; but when we do, it is not because God is wrathful, but because what He knows is the truth of things and truth may be painful. Brave indeed is the one who does not shrink from it, for none of us can bear very much reality.

Yet the best and deepest part of us longs, not only to know and bear it, but to be reconciled to it. For who among us would wish to remain false when we might be honest or avert our gaze from that which, sooner or later, we must not only acknowledge, but embrace? We know that to turn away forever from truth and reality is to suffer an enduring loss; it is to be eternally unreal, everlastingly untrue. Ask any psychiatrist.

That is why the soul will, in Plato's splendid words, "go running to judgment," not only dreading but desiring it; knowing that the flame that burns is the fire that refines; the truth that pierces is the reality that heals; the light that exposes is the brightness by which we see.

If what I have written sounds more like a defense of purgatory than a description of hell, then we should recognize that it is the only kind of "hell" that makes a theodicy possible. The eternal torment of innumerable souls is morally insupportable. Such a concept, far from forming any part of an answer to the problem of evil, would in itself present us with an indefensible evil.

"SAVED AS BY FIRE"

The doctrine of purgatory, on the other hand, is not only scriptural, but forms an indispensable part of our understanding of God's unwearied dealings with His children. Unlike belief in an endless hell, it does not constitute another problem for our understanding of God's care for His world, but becomes a valuable component of that understanding. Not only is it explicitly stated by Saint Paul in his first epistle to the Corinthians ("If any man's work shall be burned, he shall suffer loss: but he himself shall be saved; yet so as by fire."), it sustains the Apostle's reassurance of his friends in Philippi and Corinth that God will complete the good work He has started in them.

Once again, the poets help us—this time by showing us that God's creation and re-creation of us is one continuous, unbroken action whether in this life or in the life to come. John Keats—and who should know better than he?—thought that we should call this world "the vale of soul-making." Browning tells us that God's making of our souls is not limited to this temporal world, but extends to the eternal world beyond death. It, too, is a vale of soul-making. He describes purgatory as:

> That sad obscure sequestered state,
> Where God unmakes but to remake the soul
> He else made first in vain; which must not be.

What the poets have in common is their understanding that what God wishes to do with us is to make something of us. The soul is the self, the person, the character; and it is made and may be unmade and remade. And the Eternal is not limited to our "three-score years and ten" in accomplishing the good work He has begun in us.

THE FATE OF THE WICKED

But what of those who resist or refuse the unmaking and remaking of their souls? What are we to say of the fate of those who are blind because they will not see, who love illusion better than truth and darkness more than light, who persist in their impenitence and refusal to be reconciled? About the fate of the finally impenitent we wish to say five things.

First: If there be any who are finally lost, then I pray God that I not be among them, and that they be few.

Second: That God will not give any of His children up while there is anything in them that can be saved. So long as there is something to which mercy can appeal, so long the action of mercy will continue.

Third: That God will not save any who do not wish to be saved. He will not reconcile us to Himself against our will. Indeed, we should ask what it could mean to be reconciled against our will. It is for this reason that we cannot be univer-

salists. We shall not take our free will less seriously than God
does, nor treat it with less respect. He will not deny His own
nature, compelling by force at the last those whom He has all
along sought to win by love.

Fourth: Though we are not universalists, we may yet dare to
hope—indeed, who would not wish to hope—that God's mercy
will outwait, outlast, and outlove us until we wish to be reconciled to Him. He may yet be able to make us love Him, not by
forcing us to, but by bringing to bear on those He loves the
kindness of His wisdom and the action of His mercy. This is perfectly consistent with His nature. It is what He has always done.
All the penitence, faith, obedience, and love we have ever offered
to Him has been a response to the initiatives of His goodness.

Knowing God as we have seen Him in Jesus, how could we
ever believe that God's loving action on our behalf would ever
cease? And may we not be allowed to hope that finally all will
respond to it? However we think of hell, we must never allow
ourselves to believe that it is Satan's hell. It does not belong to
Satan, but to God. It is the sphere of His mercy and the realm
of His goodness.

In my native Belfast there were for many years what came to
be called "No-Go" zones, where the forces of law and order did
not enter. There are no such zones in God's providential care and
saving action. God surrenders nothing. He hands nothing over.

Fifth: We know the disintegrative power of evil. We know it
in ourselves, and we witness it in others. When we do wrong we
lose our integrity, our integration. We are no longer unified, but
have surrendered our wholeness and have begun to experience
what William James called our "torn-to-piecesness." Evil makes
us empty and robs us of substance. Any forcefulness, purpose, or
direction it may bring to us is illusory and temporary; for it carries within it the seeds of its own ruination.

We say of some people that we could put our finger through
them and meet no resistance. They are lightweights. They have

no character. When in C. S. Lewis's *The Great Divorce* visitors arrive from hell to have a look at heaven, many of them choose to return to hell because heaven is too real for them. They prefer something less definite, less substantial. Says Lewis, "A damned soul is nearly nothing: it is shrunk, shut up in itself."

Knowing this, I can imagine something of what a final disintegration might be like. It would be a loss of self, a deterioration of character and loss of identity until there was nothing left but a wisp, a wraith, a ghost of being that would no longer be aware or care—in which there would be nothing to appeal to, nothing that could see, and desire, and believe, and be saved. Says Lewis, "No soul that seriously and constantly desires joy will ever miss it." But what if there is no seriousness, constancy, or desire remaining?

ENDLESS MUSIC

When people of faith speak of the reward of heaven, they are likely to hear the criticism that believers are a selfish and mercenary lot and that the promise of heaven is nothing more than a bribe to make people religious and keep them faithful.

What critics of this sort fail to recognize is that some rewards are not only honorable, but inevitable, and there is nothing selfish about them. Heaven is not a bribe to make or keep us good; it is the dwelling-place of goodness itself. It is not a payment for walking with God, it is reaching our destination with the One who has been the Companion of our pilgrimage. It is not anything added to faith, hope, and love, but their fulfillment. It is speaking the language we have studied and singing the music we have practiced. Now, what is there that is unworthy about such an expectation and hope?

When my daughter Heather was learning to play the piano, I promised her five dollars if she would learn the first movement of Beethoven's *Moonlight* Sonata. She quickly learned it, and I promptly paid up. Her dollars were soon spent, but the sonata remained. It has stayed with her all her life. Her reward was not the money, but the music.

The reward of heaven is the music. Except that it is no longer the sound of a lone instrument, but one of a thousand, thousand blended notes in an orchestra of praise in the company of heaven. Who would not wish to learn his part and tune his instrument well?

Now I saw in my Dream, that these two men went in at the Gate; and lo! as they entered, they were transfigured; and they had raiment put on, that shone like gold. There was also that met them with harps and crowns, and gave them to them; the harps to praise withal, and the crowns in token of honour. Then I heard in my dream, that all the bells in the City rang again for joy, and that it was said unto them, *Enter ye into the joy of our Lord.* I also heard the men themselves, that they sang with a loud voice, saying, *Blessing, and honour, and glory, and power, be to him that sitteth upon the throne, and unto the Lamb, for ever and ever.*